07415066

D0618940

Family General Knowledge Quiz Book

1500 Question mixture for adults, teenagers and children

By

Catherine Galway

Copyright © 2017 by Catherine Galway
All rights reserved. No part of this book may be reproduced or transmitted in any form or by any means, electronic or mechanical, including photocopying, recording, or by any information storage and retrieval system, without the written permission of the Publisher, except where permitted by law.

Introduction

A variety of general knowledge puzzles for all age groups.

Ideal for family quiz nights, car, rail and plane journeys.

Quiz One

1. How many different letters are used in Roman numerals?
2. First published in 1969, who is the author and illustrator of the classic children's book 'The Very Hungry Caterpillar'?
3. What type of flower is worn on Remembrance Day in Britain?
4. 'I'm gonna pick up the pieces' is the opening line of which Ed Sheeran hit?
5. Pandas belong to which animal family?
6. What type of foodstuff is Monterey Jack?
7. What is the term for a period of isolation to prevent the spread of disease?
8. Neptune was the Roman god of what?
9. What were the first names of the singing Everly Brothers?
10. Which actor played the role of Captain John Miller in 'Saving Private Ryan'?
11. What are the three primary colours?
12. Who won the Academy Award for Best Actor in 2014 for his role as Stephen Hawking in 'The Theory of Everything'?
13. Which author created the fictional detective Hercule Poirot?
14. Born in June 1890 in Ulverston, England, Arthur Jefferson was the real name of which comic actor?
15. What kind of animal is a Flemish Giant?

Answers

1. Seven 2. Eric Carle 3. Poppy 4. Lego House 5. Racoon 6. Cheese 7. Quarantine 8. The Sea 9. Don and Phil 10. Tom Hanks 11. Red, blue and yellow 12. Eddie Redmayne 13. Agatha Christie 14. Stan Laurel 15. Rabbit

Quiz Two

1. 'Your beauty is beyond compare, with flaming locks of auburn hair' are lyrics from which Dolly Parton song?
2. Bucharest is the capital city of which country?
3. What is the name of the dachshund in 'The Secret Life of Pets' film?
4. Who did Paul McCartney duet with on the 1982 hit 'Ebony and Ivory'?
5. Which 17th Dutch century artist painted 'The Girl with the Pearl Earring'?
6. Chien is the French word for which animal?
7. What creatures live in a formicary?
8. In which Massachusetts Township were the famous witch trials held between February 1692 and May 1693 held?
9. Nike was the Greek goddess of what?
10. Which internet site was founded by Jimmy Wales in 2001?
11. In 'SpongeBob SquarePants' what type of creature is Gary?
12. In which month of the year is Groundhog Day celebrated in the USA?
13. In credit agreements what does the abbreviation APR stand for?
14. Hepatitis affects which organ of the human body?
15. 'The Climb' and 'Wrecking Ball' were hits for which female singer?

Answers

1. Jolene 2. Romania 3. Buddy 4. Stevie Wonder 5. Johannes Vermeer 6. Dog 7. Ants 8. Salem 9. Victory 10. Wikipedia 11. Sea snail 12. February 13. Annual Percentage Rate 14. Liver 15. Miley Cyrus

Quiz Three

1. Which male artist had a hit song in 2015 called 'Hold Back the River'?
2. The Storting is the parliament of which country?
3. In Indian cuisine what type of foodstuff is naan?
4. Which nursery rhyme character sat on and fell off a wall?
5. Which is the only state capital of the USA that has a three-word name?
6. Which English novelist wrote 'A Brave New World,' first published in 1932?
7. In 1949 David Ben-Gurion became the first prime minister of which country?
8. On the 1969 Apollo 11 mission which one of the three astronauts did not walk on the moon?
9. In a suit of armour what part of the body is protected by a casque?
10. Density, Arctic King and Little Gem are all type of what food?
11. How many valves are there on a trumpet?
12. In clothing what is a pork pie?
13. Two New York boroughs begin with B – Brooklyn and?
14. What is the maximum break in a game of snooker?
15. What was the name of the rabbit in Walt Disney's 1942 film 'Bambi'?

Answers

1. James Bay 2. Norway 3. Bread 4. Humpty Dumpty 5. Salt Lake City 6. Aldous Huxley 7. Israel 8. Michael Collins 9. Head 10. Lettuce 11. Three 12. Hat 13. Bronx 14. 147 15. Thumper

Quiz Four

1. Which American actor starred in the films 'Collateral,' 'Minority Report,' 'Rain Man' and 'Edge of Tomorrow'?
2. Kigali is the capital and largest city of which African nation?
3. Which fruit is a cross between a raspberry and a blackberry?
4. The character Ross Gellar in the television series 'Friends' was played by which actor?
5. Which nursery rhyme character 'could eat no fat'?
6. What does GPS stand for in GPS navigation devices?
7. What does a person suffering from alopecia lack?
8. According to proverb what is 'the mother of invention'?
9. Who was the oldest member of the Beatles?
10. Which tree features on the flag of Lebanon?
11. The Roadrunner is a member of which family of birds?
12. In which Parisian cemetery are Oscar Wilde, Jim Morrison and Maria Callas buried?
13. The Dolomites mountain range is located in the northeast of which country?
14. What is the name for a narrow piece of land that connects two landmasses?
15. What surname links Harry Potter actress Emma and Sherlock Holmes' narrator and sidekick John?

Answers

1. Tom Cruise 2. Rwanda 3. Loganberry 4. David Schwimmer 5. Jack Sprat 6. Global Positioning System 7. Hair 8. Necessity 9. Ringo Starr 10. Cedar 11. Cuckoo 12. Père Lachaise Cemetery 13. Italy 14. Isthmus 15. Watson

Quiz Five

1. What is the name given to the study of rocks?
2. By what name was the character Jack Dawkins better known in Charles Dickens' novel 'Oliver Twist'?
3. Which civil rights leader was assassinated on 4th April 1968?
4. What part of the human body is affected by conjunctivitis?
5. In which country did the material denim originate?
6. Who in 1983 became the first American woman in space?
7. According to the nursery rhyme, who 'ran up the hill to fetch a pail of water'?
8. What are the names of The Ghosts that chase the player in the Pac-Man video game?
9. 'Fee-fi-fo-fum, I smell the blood of an Englishman' are words from which fairy tale?
10. Which actor played Indiana's father in the 1989 film 'Indiana Jones and the Last Crusade'?
11. What was the name of the dog in Jerome K. Jerome's 1889 story 'Three Men in a Boat'?
12. What is the first line of Rupert Brooke's 1914 poem 'The Soldier'?
13. What is a male bee called?
14. What is the human pollex?
15. Which bird's name is the term given to three consecutive strikes in ten pin bowling?

Answers

1. Petrology 2. The Artful Dodger 3. Martin Luther King 4. The eyes 5. France 6. Sally Ride 7. Jack and Jill 8. Pinky, Blinky, Inky and Clyde 9. Jack and the Beanstalk 10. Sean Connery 11. Montmorency 12. If I should die, think only this of me 13. Drone 14. The thumb 15. Turkey

Quiz Six

1. Which US state used to be called the Sandwich Islands?
2. What is the name of the method of calculating runs required in a rain interrupted one day cricket match?
3. Who wrote the 1854 poem 'The Charge of The Light Brigade'?
4. Troglodytes troglodytes is the Latin name for which small bird?
5. Who in 1946 became the first Secretary-General of the United Nations?
6. Which New Zealand born pioneer of nuclear physics was the first to split the atom?
7. Which European country is nicknamed 'Country of the Thousand Lakes'?
8. At which sport was Austrian Franz Klammer a world champion?
9. Which actor played the role of Mitch Buchanan in the television series 'Baywatch'?
10. Who is Elton John's chief song writing partner?
11. What word does the 'e' in e-mail stand for?
12. Audrey Hepburn played the role of Holly Golightly in which 1961 film?
13. What is the name of the ghost in Shakespeare's play 'Macbeth'?
14. What is Paddington Bear's favourite food?
15. 'Flight,' 'Training Day' and 'The Equalizer' are films starring which two-time Academy Award winning actor?

Answers

1. Hawaii 2. Duckworth-Lewis method 3. Alfred Lord Tennyson 4. Wren 5. Trygve Lie 6. Ernest Rutherford 7. Finland 8. Skiing 9. David Hasselhoff 10. Bernie Taupin 11. Electronic 12. Breakfast at Tiffany's 13. Banquo 14. Marmalade sandwiches 15. Denzel Washington

Quiz Seven

1. Legolas in 'The Lord of the Rings' film trilogy was played by which English actor?
2. What is the title of Roald Dahl's 1972 sequel to 'Charlie and the Chocolate Factory'?
3. What is the currency of Hungary?
4. Pippi Longstocking is the title character in a series of books by which Swedish author?
5. By what name is a male witch known?
6. In the 1996 film 'Independence Day' which actor played the role of US President Thomas J Whitmore?
7. How many humps does a Bactrian camel have?
8. Which Scots-Irish mathematical physicist and engineer gave his name to the Absolute scale of temperature?
9. Poet Elizabeth Barrett married which fellow poet in 1846?
10. In which country did the Battle of Waterloo take place?
11. What event was held on Max Yasgur's farm in Bethel, New York in August 1969?
12. What was the name of the German passenger airship that crashed in New Jersey, USA on 6th May 1937?
13. In October of which year did the Cuban missile crisis take place?
14. What is the collective name for a group of witches?
15. Who was sworn in as 45th President of the United States on 20th January 2017?

Answers

1. Orlando Bloom 2. Charlie and the Great Glass Elevator 3. Forint 4. Astrid Lindgren 5. Warlock 6. Bill Pullman 7. Two 8. Kelvin 9. Robert Browning 10. Belgium 11. The Woodstock Festival 12. The Hindenburg 13. 1962 14. Coven 15. Donald Trump

Quiz Eight

1. In the nursery rhyme who 'cut off the tails of the three blind mice'?
2. Which actor won Academy Awards for his roles in 'Rain Man' and 'Kramer vs. Kramer'?
3. Which boy reporter was created by Belgian cartoonist Hergé?
4. Which sport has Greco-Roman and Freestyle as two distinct styles?
5. What is the world's most northerly capital city?
6. Which late actor played the title role in the 1998 comedy-drama film 'Patch Adams'?
7. The Portuguese city of Lisbon stands at the mouth of which river?
8. Which actor played the title role in the 1980s television series 'Remington Steele'?
9. Lupine relates to what type of animal?
10. In which country is Lake Como?
11. Who famously kept a diary in Amsterdam during World War Two?
12. What is the English translation of the Mozart opera 'Le Nozze di Figaro'?
13. Wenceslas Square is in which capital city?
14. Which organ of the body is responsible for the production of anti-bodies?
15. In trivial pursuit which colour identifies questions on geography?

Answers

1. The Farmer's wife 2. Dustin Hoffman 3. Tintin 4. Wrestling 5. Reykjavik 6. Robin Williams 7. Tagus 8. Pierce Brosnan 9. Wolf 10. Italy 11. Anne Frank 12. The Marriage of Figaro 13. Prague 14. Spleen 15. Blue

Quiz Nine

1. 'Achtung Baby' was a 1991 album release for which Irish rock band?
2. In bridge, the four players are referred to as what?
3. Which Canadian-born producer, known as the 'King of Comedy,' created the Keystone Cops?
4. Princess Poppy, Branch, Bridget and Prince Gristle are characters in which 2016 computer-animated film?
5. How many athletic events form an Olympic Decathlon?
6. Which ocean separates the United States from the United Kingdom?
7. Which planet did William Herschel discover in 1781?
8. What is the popular name for deuterium oxide?
9. What girl's name represents the letter J in the NATO phonetic alphabet?
10. What is the medical term for loss of memory?
11. 'The Soldier's Song' is the national anthem of which European country?
12. From which country does pizza originate?
13. Who was King of the United Kingdom during World War Two?
14. What tax was introduced by Peter the Great in 1698 in Russia?
15. Who in 1802 launched her first waxworks exhibition in London?

Answers

1. U2 2. North, East, South and West 3. Mack Sennett 4. Trolls
5. Ten 6. Atlantic Ocean 7. Uranus 8. Heavy water 9. Juliet
10. Amnesia 11. Republic of Ireland 12. Italy 13. George VI
14. A beard tax 15. Madame Tussaud

Quiz Ten

1. 'Use Your Illusion' was a 1991 album release for which American rock band?
2. Which actor played the role of The Riddler in the 1995 film 'Batman Forever'?
3. In which part of the body is the retina?
4. What type of dog is Mel from 'The Secret Life of Pets' film?
5. The song 'Memory' features in which musical?
6. According to the proverb, a stitch in time saves how many?
7. What was the name of the captain of the Nautilus in Jules Verne novel 'Twenty Thousand Leagues Under the Sea'?
8. Which World War Two operation was code named 'Dynamo'?
9. Which Greek philosopher wrote 'The Republic' and 'Apology?
10. V is the Roman numeral for what number?
11. Born in November 1728, what nationality was explorer Captain James Cook?
12. 'Firework' and 'The One That Got Away' were hits for which female singer?
13. Who was the President of the United States of American immediately before Barack Obama?
14. What name is given to the period of British history between 1901 and 1910?
15. Who wrote the 1922 short story that the 2008 film 'The Curious Case of Benjamin Button,' starring Brad Pitt, was based on?

Answers

1. Guns N' Roses 2. Jim Carrey 3. The eye 4. Pug 5. Cats
6. Nine 7. Nemo 8. The Dunkirk evacuation 9. Plato 10. 5
11. British 12. Katy Perry 13. George W. Bush
14. Edwardian 15. F. Scott Fitzgerald

Quiz Eleven

1. 'The Lass that Loved a Sailor' is the alternative title of which Gilbert & Sullivan comic opera of 1878?
2. 'Two roads diverged in a yellow wood' is the first line of which 1916 poem by Robert Frost?
3. What animal is the symbol of the Democratic Party in the USA?
4. Which former electrician won the Nobel Peace Prize in 1983?
5. In Greek mythology, who was the God of Dreams?
6. What is a fandango?
7. What is a line on a weather map that connects points of equal temperatures called?
8. What type of food is porcini?
9. What were the names of the hecklers in 'The Muppet Show'?
10. Of which girl group was Kelly Rowland a member?
11. What name was given to the Supreme Court of ancient Rome?
12. What was the classical standard language of ancient India?
13. In the television series 'Frasier' what was the name of Martin Crane's pet dog?
14. What is the opposite of convex?
15. What liquid measure is equal to 1.76 imperial pints?

Answers

1. H.M.S. Pinafore 2. The Road Not Taken 3. Donkey 4. Lech Walesa 5. Morpheus 6. Dance 7. Isotherm 8. Mushrooms 9. Statler and Waldorf 10. Destiny's Child 11. The Senate 12. Sanskrit 13. Eddie 14. Concave 15. Litre

Quiz Twelve

1. Dorothy Zbornak, Rose Nylund and Blanche Devereaux were characters in which American sitcom?
2. What colour of caps are worn by the Australian national cricket team?
3. 'The Mask,' 'The Holiday' and 'Gangs of New York,' are films starring which actress?
4. Which novel features extracts from the diary of Jonathan Harker?
5. Drawn up in 1867, the Queensberry Rules which apply to which sport?
6. How many different pieces can be found on a chess board?
7. Alpine, Angora and Toggenburg are all breeds of which animal?
8. Pontoon and cantilever are both types of which construction?
9. What is the name of an angle which is less than 90 degrees?
10. Which 2016 Little Mix song features Sean Paul?
11. What type of puppets are those whose movements are controlled by wires or strings?
12. First performed in 1952, who wrote the murder mystery play 'The Mousetrap'?
13. What is the last letter of the Greek alphabet?
14. What type of animal is a silverback?
15. Julius was the real name of which of the Marx Brothers?

Answers

1. The Golden Girls 2. Green 3. Cameron Diaz 4. Dracula
5. Boxing 6. Six 7. Goat 8. Bridge 9. Acute 10. Hair
11. Marionettes 12. Agatha Christie 13. Omega 14. Gorilla
15. Groucho

Quiz Thirteen

1. 'Bat Out of Hell' was a 1977 album release for which American rock singer?
2. How many sides does an octagon have?
3. Which English computer scientist invented the World Wide Web?
4. Which British surgeon, born in April 1827, was a pioneer of antiseptic surgery?
5. In which country are Mariachi bands traditional?
6. What is the name of Yogi Bear's girlfriend?
7. Which size of paper measures 210 mm x 297 mm?
8. How many animals are used to designate the years of the Chinese calendar?
9. What is the brightest planet in the night sky?
10. How many strings does a mandolin have?
11. In which city is the Manneken Pis fountain?
12. George W Bush governor of which state before becoming President of the United States?
13. 'Old Copper nose' was the nickname of which King of England who reigned from 1509 until 1547?
14. Which English city is known as 'City of Dreaming Spires'?
15. What does the acronym NASA stand for?

Answers

1. Meat Loaf 2. Eight 3. Tim Berners-Lee 4. Joseph Lister 5. Mexico 6. Cindy Bear 7. A4 8. 12 9. Venus 10. Eight 11. Brussels 12. Texas 13. Henry VIII 14. Oxford 15. National Aeronautics and Space Administration

Quiz Fourteen

1. Which Mediterranean island was awarded the George Cross in 1942?
2. What dinosaur had a name meaning three-horned face?
3. Which Pope served from 26th August 1978 until his sudden death 33 days later?
4. During the time of Augustus Caesar the year began in which month?
5. In the television sitcom ‘Friends’ what was Joey’s surname?
6. In the cartoon series ‘Wacky Races’ which who drove the Compact Pussycat?
7. How many years of marriage are celebrated by a Golden Wedding Anniversary?
8. What gas makes soda water fizz?
9. Which Olympic sport needs a planting box?
10. What natural disasters are ranked in severity by the Saffir-Simpson scale?
11. What is the speech at the beginning of a play called?
12. The first woman to serve as United States Attorney General died 7th November 2016. What was her name?
13. ‘The Laughing Cavalier’ is a 1624 Baroque portrait by which Dutch painter?
14. With an elevation of 3,798 m / 12,461 ft Grossglockner is the highest mountain in which European country?
15. Georgios Kyriacos Panayiotou is the real name of which late English singer/songwriter, who died in December 2016?

Answers

1. Malta 2. Triceratops 3. John Paul I 4. March 5. Tribbiani
6. Penelope Pitstop 7. 50 8. Carbon dioxide 9. Pole vault
10. Hurricanes 11. Prologue 12. Janet Reno 13. Frans Hals
14. Austria 15. George Michael

Quiz Fifteen

1. The River Murray is the longest river in which country?
2. Who won the Academy Award for Best Actress in 2016 for her role as Mia Dolan in ‘La La Land’?
3. What word is the name given to the dried kernel of a coconut?
4. Mount Everest stands on the border of which two countries?
5. Which female artist released a song called ‘Needed Me’ in 2016?
6. In 1800 which Italian physicist invented the first true battery?
7. What is the name of Doc Brown’s dog in ‘Back to the Future’?
8. Masked, hermit and spider are all types of which creature?
9. What is the name given to a baby kangaroo?
10. What was the former name of Cape Canaveral?
11. What is the full moon nearest the autumnal equinox called?
12. What is the literal English translation of the French phrase ‘cordon bleu’?
13. What is the name of the bacterium that causes food poisoning in contaminated food?
14. What is the capital of Nepal?
15. What type of panda is Master Shifu from ‘Kung Fu Panda’?

Answers

1. Australia 2. Emma Stone 3. Copra 4. Nepal and Tibet
5. Rihanna 6. Alessandro Volta 7. Einstein 8. Crab 9. Joey
10. Cape Kennedy 11. Harvest moon 12. Blue ribbon
13. Salmonella 14. Kathmandu 15. Red

Quiz Sixteen

1. Kerkyra is the Greek name for which island?
2. During World War Two what was the code name for the Allied invasion of Europe?
3. Rene Descartes' 1637 quote 'Cogito ergo sum' means what in English?
4. Who wrote the 1982 science fiction novel 'The Running Man' under the pseudonym Richard Bachman?
5. Who won the Academy Award for Best Director in 1963 for the film 'Lawrence of Arabia'?
6. In the nursery rhyme what did the three little kittens lose?
7. What gas in the blood of divers can cause 'the bends'?
8. What type of medical professional is an ophthalmologist?
9. What name is given to the soft spot on top of a baby's head?
10. What title is given to the head of state of Kuwait?
11. On a ship what is housed in a binnacle?
12. Which female artist released a 2015 song called 'Kill Em With Kindness'?
13. How many centimetres are there in one metre?
14. What type of insect does a chrysalis turn into?
15. In Egypt, the Sphinx has the head of a human being and the body of which animal?

Answers

1. Corfu 2. Operation Overlord 3. I think therefore I am
4. Stephen King 5. David Lean 6. Their mittens 7. Nitrogen
8. Eye doctor 9. Fontanelle 10. Emir 11. Compass
12. Selena Gomez 13. 100 14. Butterfly 15. Lion

Quiz Seventeen

1. What do tadpoles turn into?
2. Cocoa Beach was the location of which 1960s sitcom starring Larry Hagman and Barbara Eden?
3. What aquatic weasel lives in a holt?
4. What is the Mexican avocado dip flavoured with lime, coriander and spice called?
5. The Yucatan Channel separates which two countries?
6. What is the name of the vehicle used to clean and smooth off the ice on an ice rink?
7. What name is shared by a breed of duck and a shade of dark greenish blue?
8. Which actor won the Academy Award for Best Actor in 1981 for his role in 'On Golden Pond'?
9. The Vikings used an alphabet consisting of 16 symbols, known as what?
10. What do galvanised iron sheets have a coating of?
11. In 1997 which comet came within 125 million miles of Earth?
12. Is the Sun a planet or a star?
13. Which three sports make up a triathlon?
14. In the Soviet Union who did Yuri Andropov succeed in 1984?
15. What is the largest species of antelope?

Answers

1. Frogs 2. I Dream of Jeannie 3. Otter 4. Guacamole 5. Cuba and Mexico 6. Zamboni 7. Teal 8. Henry Fonda 9. Runes 10. Zinc 11. Hale-Bopp 12. Star 13. Swimming, cycling and running 14. Leonid Brezhnev 15. Eland

Quiz Eighteen

1. How many pockets are there on a snooker table?
2. Russia spans which two continents?
3. Which device measures the speed of wind?
4. Who sang the theme song to the 2012 James Bond film 'Skyfall'?
5. Ally Brooke, Normani Kordei, Dinah Jane and Lauren Jauregui are members of which American group?
6. Which sport uses the lightest ball?
7. By what name is Schubert`s Symphony No. 8 better known?
8. What is the national bird of India?
9. Uluru is the aboriginal name for which Australian landmark?
10. Which actor is the father of Angelina Jolie?
11. Joe Strummer was the lead singer of which punk band?
12. What is the actual colour of the black box flight recorder in commercial aircraft?
13. From which language does the word alphabet derive?
14. How many finger holes are there on the front of a recorder?
15. Which continent has the most countries in the world?

Answers

1. Six 2. Europe and Asia 3. Anemometer 4. Adele 5. Fifth Harmony 6. Table tennis 7. Unfinished Symphony 8. Peacock 9. Ayers Rock 10. Jon Voight 11. The Clash 12. Orange 13. Greek 14. Seven 15. Africa

Quiz Nineteen

1. What type of natural disaster can be described as a series of sea waves caused by an earthquake or volcanic eruption?
2. Greece is located on which continent?
3. How many eyelids do camels have on each eye?
4. Which author wrote the novel 'Les Miserables'?
5. What is the name of the dog in Punch and Judy?
6. What type of creature is a gecko?
7. Which One Direction band member released a 2016 song called 'Pillowtalk'?
8. Which series of action films features a police detective called Martin Riggs?
9. Which series of animated films feature a woolly mammoth called Manny?
10. What are competitors required to hold in a game of kabaddi?
11. What is a young hare called?
12. How many basic positions of the feet are there in ballet?
13. In the human body what does lacrimal fluid lubricate?
14. On which river does the Irish city of Dublin stand?
15. Which beverage is used to flavour the Italian dessert Tiramisu?

Answers

1. Tsunami 2. Europe 3.Three 4. Victor Hugo 5. Toby 6. Lizard
7. Zayn Malik 8. Lethal Weapon 9. Ice Age 10. Their breath
11. Leveret 12. Five 13. Eyes 14. Liffey 15. Coffee

Quiz Twenty

1. Which male singer had a 2015 hit song with 'Love Yourself'?
2. Which is the smallest independent state in the world?
3. The name of which flower derives from the Turkish for turban?
4. Ailurophobia is the fear of which type of animal?
5. What does the Italian word antipasti mean?
6. What was the name of Russia's first permanently manned space station?
7. Which Australian actor starred in the films 'The Wolverine,' 'Prisoners,' 'X-Man Origins: Wolverine,' and 'Van Helsing?'
8. How many toes does an ostrich have on one foot?
9. In which decade of the 20th century was the Spanish Civil War?
10. Which is the closest African country to the Spanish mainland?
11. Who wrote the musical 'Blood Brothers'?
12. What name is given to the attempt to turn base metals into gold?
13. Which English scientist and engineer invented the bouncing bomb, used in the 'Dambusters' raid to attack the dams of the Ruhr Valley during World War II?
14. Doha is the capital city of which country?
15. Which female singer features in Drake's 2016 song 'Too good?'

Answers

1. Justin Bieber 2. Vatican City 3. Tulip 4. Cat 5. Before the meal 6. MIR 7. Hugh Jackman 8. Two 9. 1930s 10. Morocco 11. Willy Russell 12. Alchemy 13. Barnes Wallis 14. Qatar 15. Rihanna

Quiz Twenty One

1. Sheldon, Leonard, Howard and Raj are characters in which American television sitcom?
2. Mount Aneto is the highest peak in which Spanish range of mountains?
3. Which gas is produced in the Haber process?
4. Which Italian explorer arrived in Cuba in 1492?
5. What colour is the breast of a robin?
6. Which actors played the title roles in the 1966 film 'The Good, The Bad and the Ugly'?
7. 'Jude the Obscure' was the last novel of which British author?
8. In which year of World War Two did the Japanese bomb Pearl Harbor?
9. Which cartoon character is described as 'the fastest mouse in all Mexico'?
10. What is tested using a Snellen chart?
11. The name of which car manufacturer derives from the Latin for "I roll"?
12. What is grown in a paddy field?
13. Who wrote the 1994 novel 'Captain Corelli's Mandolin'?
14. Which stringed instrument is plucked with a mezrāb or zakhmeh?
15. Who is the Greek God of the Sea?

Answers

1. The Big Bang Theory 2. Pyrenees 3. Ammonia 4. Christopher Columbus 5. Red 6. Clint Eastwood, Lee Van Cleef, Eli Wallach 7. Thomas Hardy 8. 1941 9. Speedy Gonzales 10. Eyesight 11. Volvo 12. Rice 13. Louis de Bernieres 14. Sitar 15. Poseidon

Quiz Twenty Two

1. Which mythological creature has the upper body of a human and the lower body of a horse?
2. 'Blazing Saddles,' The Producers' and 'Stir Crazy' are films starring which actor, who died 29th August 2016?
3. Which 1964 musical features the song 'The Rain in Spain'?
4. Siam was the former name of which country?
5. Which British author wrote 'Day of the Jackal'?
6. 'Hakuna Matata' is a song from which Disney film?
7. In medicine what device is used to measure lung capacity?
8. What is the name of the highest peak in New Zealand?
9. Which two word Latin phrase is used as an acknowledgement of one's fault or error?
10. How is the vitamin Riboflavin also known?
11. A shearwater is what type of creature?
12. Which spice is obtained from the outer shell of nutmeg?
13. What name was given to the memorial garden dedicated to John Lennon in New York's Central Park?
14. Which Clement Clarke Moore poem opens with the line, 'Twas the night before Christmas'?
15. What is the national flower of Japan?

Answers

1. Centaur 2. Gene Wilder 3. My Fair Lady 4. Thailand 5. Frederick Forsyth 6. Lion King 7. Spirometer 8. Mount Cook 9. Mea culpa 10. Vitamin B2 11. Seabird 12. Mace 13. Strawberry Fields 14. A Visit from St Nicholas 15. Chrysanthemum

Quiz Twenty Three

1. How many interlocking rings are there on the Olympic flag?
2. In the tale of Snow White which of the seven dwarfs was beardless?
3. How many pawns are on a chessboard at the start of play?
4. What is the name of the Nanny played by Emma Thompson in two films in 2005 and 2010?
5. Margaret Page and Alice Ford are the title characters in which Shakespeare play?
6. What is the more common name for solid carbon dioxide?
7. What was the former name of Mali?
8. Which Academy Award winning actor played the role of Rooster Cogburn in the 2010 re-make of 'True Grit'?
9. Artemis was the twin sister of which Greek god?
10. What is the name of the mountain pass that forms a border between Italy and Austria?
11. Revolutionary, guerrilla leader and diplomat Che Guevara was born in 1928 in which country?
12. From which bird is pâté de foie gras produced?
13. Who was the author of 1925 novel 'The Great Gatsby'?
14. Who won the Academy Award for Best Actor in 2015 for his role as Hugh Glass in 'The Revenant'?
15. In the Harry Potter books what is the name of the ghost who haunts the first-floor girls' bathroom?

Answers

1. Five 2. Dopey 3. 16 4. Nanny McPhee 5. The Merry Wives of Windsor 6. Dry Ice 7. French Sudan 8. Jeff Bridges 9. Apollo 10. Brenner Pass 11. Argentina 12. Goose 13. F Scott Fitzgerald 14. Leonardo DiCaprio 15. Moaning Myrtle

Quiz Twenty Four

1. What is the main artery of the human body, which supplies oxygenated blood to the circulatory system?
2. 'The Rake's Progress' is the most famous painting of which English painter?
3. Glenn Frey died 18th January 2016; he was a founding member of which band, whose hits include 'Hotel California'?
4. Who took the name Sebastian Melmoth when living in impoverished exile in Paris?
5. Who won the Academy Award for Best Actress in 2010 for her role as Nina Sayers in 'Black Swan'?
6. Valentino Rossi was a nine-time world champion in which sport?
7. Lyndon B Johnson served as vice-president to whom?
8. Which nuts are used in a Waldorf salad?
9. State Duma is the lower house of which country's parliament?
10. What is the world's northernmost capital city?
11. What name is given to a baby whale?
12. What is the chemical name for quicklime?
13. What type of animal is Akela in Rudyard Kipling's 'The Jungle Book'?
14. What is measured using the Beaufort Scale?
15. How is the sport of ping pong also known?

Answers

1. Aorta 2. William Hogarth. 3. The Eagles 4. Oscar Wilde
5. Natalie Portman 6. MotoGP 7. President John F. Kennedy
8. Walnuts 9. Russia 10. Reykjavík 11. Calf 12. Calcium oxide
13. Wolf 14. Wind speed 15. Table tennis

Quiz Twenty Five

1. The Cole Porter musical ‘Kiss Me Kate’ is based on which Shakespeare play?
2. How is Hansen’s Disease more commonly known?
3. What is the world’s largest rodent?
4. In which sport does the net stand 2.43 m high?
5. Which television series was set in the fictional town of Cabot Cove, Maine?
6. In the 1996 film musical ‘Evita’, who played Juan Peron opposite Madonna as Eva?
7. Which is the largest of the Balearic Islands?
8. What part of the human body is a nephrologist concerned with?
9. How many tentacles does an octopus have?
10. In cartoons which cat is the archenemy of Tweety Pie?
11. In Roman mythology Mars was the god of what?
12. What name is given to a baby owl?
13. What instrument did jazz musician Louis Armstrong?
14. Cu is the chemical symbol for what?
15. What fantasy game is known as D and D?

Answers

1. The Taming Of The Shrew 2. Leprosy 3. Capybara 4. Volleyball 5. Murder, She Wrote 6. Jonathan Pryce 7. Majorca 8. Kidneys 9. Eight 10. Sylvester 11. War 12. Owlet 13. Trumpet 14. Copper 15. Dungeons and Dragons

Quiz Twenty Six

1. Written in 1741, the English-language oratorio ‘Messiah’ was a work by which German born composer?
2. ‘Mr & Mrs Clark and Percy’ is a painting by which British artist?
3. What is the study of bird’s eggs called?
4. In Greek mythology who was killed by a poisoned arrow in his heel?
5. Who, in 1969, became the first man on the moon?
6. My momma always said, ‘Life was like a box of chocolates. You never know what you’re gonna get,’ is a quote from which Tom Hanks’ film?
7. What does the acronym CIA stand for?
8. Which fruit is used to make a Banoffee Pie?
9. What colour jersey is worn by the winners of each stage of the Tour De France?
10. In the third Harry Potter novel, who is the prisoner of Azkaban?
11. Cirrus or cumulus are examples of what?
12. A millennium celebrates the anniversary of how many years?
13. What name is given to a female ferret?
14. Which is the highest mountain in Africa?
15. ‘Mmmbop’ was a 1997 hit for which American pop band?

Answers

1. George Frideric Handel 2. David Hockney 3. Oology 4. Achilles 5. Neil Armstrong 6. Forrest Gump 7. Central Intelligence Agency 8. Banana 9. Yellow 10. Sirius Black 11. Clouds 12. 1000 13. A jill 14. Kilimanjaro 15. Hanson

Quiz Twenty Seven

1. What is the name of Marlins wife and Nemo's mother in 'Finding Nemo'?
2. What is the longest bone in the human body?
3. What is someone who shoes horses called?
4. Where in Cornwall is the most southerly point on mainland Great Britain?
5. Who played the role of Dr Raymond Stantz in the 1984 film 'Ghostbusters'?
6. Thick seam, honeycomb and blanket are all types of what food?
7. What word is French for 'thank you'?
8. In ancient history, a Pharaoh was a ruler in which country?
9. What are molars, premolars, incisors and canines all types of?
10. From what tree do acorns come?
11. If you were born on Christmas day under what zodiac sign would you be?
12. Which is the nearest country to the North Pole?
13. In which Indian city is the Taj Mahal located?
14. Which planet is known as The Red Planet?
15. In netball for what does WA stand?

Answers

1. Coral 2. Femur 3. Farrier 4. Lizard Point 5. Dan Aykroyd 6. Tripe 7. Merci 8. Egypt 9. Teeth 10. Oak 11. Capricorn 12. Greenland 13. Agra 14. Mars 15. Wing Attack

Quiz Twenty Eight

1. What eight-letter word is the name given to a five-line poem?
2. Who wrote the 1957 book 'The Grinch That Stole Christmas'?
3. What is the German parliament known as?
4. Which North African city has a name that means 'white house' in Spanish?
5. How many months of the year have 31 days?
6. 'My Coo Ca Choo' and 'Jealous Mind' were hits for which English singer, who died in 2014?
7. What term is used in tennis for a score of 40-40?
8. Tic-Tac-Toe is an alternative name for which game?
9. What is the largest planet in the solar system?
10. Feline means relating to what sort of animal?
11. In which sport would someone perform a slam dunk?
12. Which sea separates Europe and Africa?
13. What organs enable fish to breathe under water?
14. Which opera was composed by Giuseppe Verdi to commemorate the opening of the Suez Canal, was first performed on 24th December 1871?
15. What is a young goat called?

Answers

1. Limerick 2. Dr Seuss 3. Bundestag 4. Casablanca 5. Seven 6. Alvin Stardust 7. Deuce 8. Noughts and Crosses 9. Jupiter 10. Cat 11. Basketball 12. The Mediterranean 13. Gills 14. Aida 15. Kid

Quiz Twenty Nine

1. What is the term for something that will break down naturally?
2. In the Harry Potter books and films what is the name of his pet owl?
3. In the USA what is an estate agent known as?
4. How many red stripes are there on the flag of the USA?
5. What currency is used in Japan?
6. What is the name of the fictional English archaeologist in the video game 'Tomb Raider'?
7. Which Shakespeare play features the Montague and Capulet families?
8. In 1875, who became the first man to swim the English Channel?
9. What type of domestic appliance was patented by Kenneth Wood in 1950?
10. In which ocean are the Falkland Islands?
11. How many cents is the US coin the Nickel worth?
12. What type of animal is a lynx?
13. In English, what name is given to a word or phrase that reads the same backwards as it does forwards?
14. Which Shakespeare play contains the famous speech beginning: 'To be or not to be'?
15. What type of dog breed is a Jack Russell?

Answers

1. Biodegradable 2. Hedwig 3. Realtor 4. Seven 5. Yen
6. Lara Croft 7. Romeo and Juliet 8. Matthew Webb
9. Food mixer 10. Atlantic 11. Five 12. Cat
13. Palindrome 14. Hamlet 15. Terrier

Quiz Thirty

1. Who wrote the novels 'The Time Machine' and 'The Invisible Man'?
2. A cavy is another name for which domestic rodent?
3. From what country does Lego come?
4. What is the name of Eoin Colfer's teenage criminal mastermind?
5. What is the smallest planet in the solar system?
6. What is the total of the numbers on a clock face?
7. Which city in the south of France is famous for its annual film festival?
8. Which chess piece is the smallest in size and value?
9. Micky Dolenz, Michael Nesmith, Peter Tork and Davy Jones were members of which 1960s band?
10. What's the official language of Argentina?
11. In the Star Wars films which actor provides the voice of Darth Vader?
12. What was the first name of Beatrix Potter's character Puddle-Duck?
13. What is the title of the United States of America's national anthem?
14. 'Knight and Day,' 'Edge of Tomorrow' and 'Top Gun' are films starring which actor?
15. Zeta is the sixth letter of which alphabet?

Answers

1. H. G. Wells 2. Guinea pig 3. Denmark 4. Artemis Fowl
5. Mercury 6. 78 7. Cannes 8. Pawn 9. The Monkees
10. Spanish 11. James Earl Jones 12. Jemima 13. The Star-Spangled Banner 14. Tom Cruise 15.Greek

Quiz Thirty One

1. The Matterhorn is in which range of mountains?
2. What is the capital city of the US state of Arkansas?
3. What is a beaver's home called?
4. W. G. Grace was an English amateur cricketer; what was his profession?
5. Under what penname did Eric Arthur Blair write?
6. Which actor won Academy Awards for his roles in the two films 'Hannah and her Sisters' and 'The Cider House Rules'?
7. English engineer Christopher Cockerell was best known as the inventor of which form of transport?
8. What is a Blenheim Orange?
9. Which Ukrainian town was the site of a catastrophic nuclear accident on 26th April 1986?
10. What name is given to vegetarians who will not eat any food of animal origin such as eggs, milk or cheese?
11. At the Summer Olympic Games, athletes from which country traditionally enter first and lead the parade?
12. Which pop singer had a global 1991 hit with '(Everything I Do) I Do It For You'?
13. How many sides does a dodecagon have?
14. Which musical instrument has a German name that translates into English as 'bell play'?
15. Which character did Jodie Foster play in the 1991 film 'Silence of the Lambs'?

Answers

1. The Alps 2. Little Rock 3. Lodge 4. Physician 5. George Orwell 6. Michael Caine 7. Hovercraft 8. Apple 9. Chernobyl 10.Vegans 11. Greece 12 Bryan Adams 13. Twelve 14. Glockenspiel 15.Clarice Starling

Quiz Thirty Two

1. In Rudyard Kipling's 'The Jungle Book' what was the name of the tiger?
2. The Vandellas were the backing group of which singer?
3. How many legs do insects have?
4. What was the scientific formula H20?
5. Gato is the Spanish word for which animal?
6. What is the Italian name for Rome?
7. Who was the Lady with the Lamp during the Crimean War?
8. Pixel is a shortened version of which two words?
9. What name given to the inner tower of a castle?
10. Who wrote stories about Flopsy, Mopsy and Cottontail?
11. Which Italian city is famous for its canals?
12. Which musical instrument was invented by Belgian Adolphe Sax in 1846?
13. What is the name of the Japanese style of wrestling and Japan's national sport?
14. What are the only two countries to have a land border with the USA?
15. What was the name of the character played by Elizabeth Montgomery in the television series 'Bewitched'?

Answers

1. Shere Khan 2. Martha Reeves 3. Six 4. Water 5. Cat 6. Roma
7. Florence Nightingale 8. Picture element 9. Keep
10. Beatrix Potter 11.Venice 12. Saxophone 13. Sumo
14. Canada and Mexico 15. Samantha Stephens

Quiz Thirty Three

1. Which children's writer created the character Noddy?
2. What game is played on a lawn called a crown green?
3. What type of animal are pinto, haflinger and shire?
4. In poetry how many lines are in a quatrain?
5. To which island was Napoleon banished to in 1814?
6. Which country was ruled by the Valois dynasty from 1328 to 1589?
7. What is the pirate's flag with the skull and cross-bones called?
8. Which Italian artist painted The Mona Lisa?
9. A fish represents which sign of the zodiac?
10. What is the chemical symbol for gold?
11. In alphabetical order, what are the first three states of the USA?
12. Who played Clark Kent/Superman in the 2013 film 'Man of Steel'?
13. Juan Carlos I reigned as King of which country from 1975 until his abdication in 2014?
14. What letter of the alphabet appears on the cold-water taps in France?
15. What is a chicken less than sixth months old called?

Answers

1. Enid Blyton 2. Bowls 3. Horse 4. Four 5. Elba 6. France
7. Jolly Roger 8. Leonardo Da Vinci 9. Pisces 10. Au
11. Alabama, Alaska, Arizona 12. Henry Cavill 13. Spain 14. F
15. Pullet

Quiz Thirty Four

1. Morrissey is the lead singer of which indie rock band?
2. What is the capital city of New Zealand?
3. Which Italian city has a famous leaning tower?
4. Which flower is also the name of the Greek goddess of the rainbow?
5. In legend which city was besieged for 10 years by a Greek army led by King Agamemnon?
6. What number is represented by the letters XIX in Roman numerals?
7. 'Für Elise,' 'Symphony No.9' and 'Fidelio' are works by which German composer?
8. What is the more usual name for the polygraph?
9. What is the name for the organism on which a parasite lives and feeds?
10. Which planet in the solar system is closest to the Sun?
11. What is the more common name for the olfactory organ?
12. Which English novelist published works under the pen name Ellis Bell?
13. Where is the ocean of storms?
14. Sidney Poitier played the role of Virgil Tibbs in which Academy Award winning 1967 film?
15. A Rhode Island Red is a breed of what?

Answers

1. The Smiths 2. Wellington 3. Pisa 4. Iris 5. Troy 6. 19
7. Ludwig van Beethoven 8. Lie detector 9. Host 10. Mercury
11. Nose 12. Emily Bronte 13. On the moon 14. In The Heat of the Night 15. Chicken

Quiz Thirty Five

1. Which comic character has a dog called Gnasher?
2. What type of creature is a sidewinder?
3. In human anatomy, what is the more common name for the trachea?
4. In which African country is the town of Timbuktu?
5. From which flower is vanilla extracted?
6. Which is the only US state beginning with the letter L?
7. There are how many sides on a pentagon?
8. In which US town did the Gunfight at the O.K. Corral take place on 26th October 1881?
9. What word describes a person who lacks skin pigment?
10. What was the name of Leonardo DiCaprio's character in the 1997 film 'Titanic'?
11. What is the nationality of the four-time Formula One champion Sebastian Vettel?
12. What is the first name of American lexicographer Webster, who published a dictionary still used today?
13. Beneath which Paris monument is the tomb of France's unknown soldier?
14. 'Waiting for Godot' and 'Happy Days' are works by which Irish playwright, who was awarded the Novel Prize for Literature in 1969?
15. 'Leader of the Pack' was a 1960s hit for which American girl pop group?

Answers

1. Dennis the Menace 2. Snake 3. Windpipe 4. Mali 5. Orchid
6. Louisiana 7. Five 8. Tombstone 9. Albino 10. Jack Dawson
11. German 12. Noah 13. Arc de Triomphe 14. Samuel Beckett
15. The Shangri-Las

Quiz Thirty Six

1. What word derived from the German language means the double of a living person?
2. In which ancient religion was Huitzilopochtli a deity of war and sun?
3. Instituted in 1943 what is the animal equivalent of the Victoria Cross?
4. Wackford Squeers is a headmaster in which Charles Dickens' novel?
5. Paul David Hewson is the real name of which rock star, born 10th May 1960 in Dublin, Republic of Ireland?
6. Who lives in a dustbin on 'Sesame Street'?
7. In mobile phone and tablet use, what is 'app' short for?
8. Which girl band released a hit song in 2015 called 'Black Magic'?
9. What is the white part of an egg called?
10. What make of car is a Carrera?
11. What words both 'hello' and 'goodbye' in Hawaii?
12. Which drug is named after the Greek God of Dreams?
13. On which continent are the Appalachian Mountains?
14. Jamie Foxx and Colin Farrell starred in which 2006 film, a big screen remake of a 1980s television series?
15. What is the capital city of Morocco?

Answers

1. Doppelgänger 2. Aztec 3. The Dickin Medal 4. Nicholas Nickleby 5. Bono 6. Oscar the Grouch 7. Application 8. Little Mix 9. Albumen 10. Porsche 11. Aloha 12. Morphine 13. North America 14. Miami Vice 15. Rabat

Quiz Thirty Seven

1. Who wrote the 1924 novel ‘Beau Geste’?
2. What is the capital of Australia’s Northern Territory?
3. In the 1994 animated film ‘The Lion King’ which actor voiced the villainous lion Scar?
4. What is included in a BLT sandwich?
5. Which European city was known as Kristiania from 1877 to 1925?
6. The French Foreign Legion was founded in 1831 in which country?
7. The theme to ‘The Lone Ranger’ in radio, television and film comes from the overture to which opera?
8. ‘I must go down to the seas again’ is the opening line of which John Masefield 1902 poem?
9. Which English novelist wrote the 1956 book ‘The Hundred and One Dalmatians’?
10. What is the common name for sodium bicarbonate?
11. Which band had a hit with ‘Cake by the Ocean’ in 2015?
12. In which country is the source of the River Amazon located?
13. In mythology which King of Cyprus fell in love with an ivory statue of the goddess Aphrodite?
14. ‘Sverige’ appears on the postage stamps of which country?
15. Keith Flint is the vocalist of which band?

Answers

1. P. C. Wren 2. Darwin 3. Jeremy Irons 4. Bacon, lettuce and tomato 5. Oslo 6. Algeria 7. William Tell Overture 8. Sea Fever 9. Dodie Smith 10. Baking soda 11. DNCE 12. Peru 13. Pygmalion 14. Sweden 15. The Prodigy

Quiz Thirty Eight

1. Who invented the thermometer?
2. What is the common name of Sirius the brightest star in the sky?
3. Which vegetable did Gregor Mendel use when experimenting with genetics?
4. Which rapper released a song in 2015 called 'See You Again'?
5. What word is the opposite of evergreen?
6. What is cryptology the study of?
7. What colour is the maple leaf on the flag of Canada?
8. First published in 1995, who wrote the memoir 'Dreams from My Father'?
9. Which school of architecture and design did Walter Gropius found in 1919?
10. What was the name of the granodiorite stele that became the key for deciphering ancient Egyptian hieroglyphics?
11. What is the more common name for the wood hyacinth?
12. In the Mr. Men series, what colour is Mr. Tickle?
13. Which title is given to the wife of a Duke?
14. In Indian cuisine what is ghee?
15. Which author, who died in 2001, wrote 'The Hitchhiker's Guide to the Galaxy'?

Answers

1. Galileo Galilei 2. Dog Star 3. Peas 4. Wiz Khalifa
5. Deciduous 6. Codes 7. Red 8. Barack Obama 9. Bauhaus
10. Rosetta Stone 11. Bluebell 12. Orange 13. Duchess
14. Clarified butter 15. Douglas Adams

Quiz Thirty Nine

1. In which part of the human body is the brachial artery?
2. Robin Williams played DJ Adrian Cronauer in which 1987 comedy-drama film?
3. Which two creatures are depicted on the coat of arms of Australia?
4. Which is the most abundant element in our universe?
5. Guglielmo was the first name of which Italian inventor and electrical engineer known for his pioneering work on long-distance radio transmission?
6. Which female artist had a 2015 hit song with ‘Hello’?
7. In a game of darts what is the highest possible score using three darts?
8. ‘To infinity and beyond’ is the catchphrase of which animated character?
9. Which former actor was elected Governor of the US state of California in 1966?
10. How many chambers are there in the human heart?
11. From which country does the dish Goulash originate?
12. Which country did Lennox Lewis represent when he won an Olympic boxing gold medal?
13. Which author wrote the novel ‘Dr Zhivago’?
14. Pollen is produced in what part of a flower?
15. Tallahassee is the capital city of which US state?

Answers

1. Arm 2. Good Morning, Vietnam 3. Kangaroo and emu 4. Hydrogen 5. Marconi 6. Adele 7. 180 8. Buzz Lightyear 9. Ronald Reagan 10. Four 11. Hungary 12. Canada 13. Boris Pasternak 14. Anther 15. Florida

Quiz Forty

1. The currency escudo was replaced in which country by the Euro?
2. Who did Priscilla Ann Wagner marry in 1967?
3. Which Australian city was named after the wife of William IV?
4. Which unit of measurement is equivalent to 4,840 sq yards?
5. What is the present-day name for a camelopard?
6. Quint, Martin Brody and Matt Hooper were the three main characters in which 1975 blockbuster?
7. What is the name of the girlfriend of Mickey Mouse?
8. In the human body what is the more common name for myeloid tissue?
9. Which king of England, who reigned from 1272 to 1307, was known as the Hammer of the Scots?
10. What English county has been called the 'Garden of England'?
11. Who won the Eurovision Song Contest for Switzerland in 1988, with the song 'Ne partez pas sans moi'?
12. By what name is the film industry of Mumbai known?
13. Which American rapper released an album in 2016 called 'The Life of Pablo'?
14. What is the name of New York's stock exchange?
15. The name of which former capital city of Japan is an anagram of the present day capital?

Answers

1. Portugal 2. Elvis Presley 3 Adelaide 4. Acre 5. Giraffe
6. Jaws 7. Minnie Mouse 8. Bone marrow 9. Edward I
10. Kent 11. Céline Dion 12. Bollywood 13. Kanye West
14. Dow Jones Index 15. Kyoto

Quiz Forty One

1. By what other name is William Wordsworth's 1807 'I wandered lonely as a cloud' poem known?
2. Mrs Malaprop is a character in which 1775 play by Richard Brinsley Sheridan?
3. The 2006 film 'The Last King of Scotland,' starring Forest Whitaker, was about which African dictator?
4. 'Parallel Lines' was a 1978 album release for which American rock band?
5. Rothschild, Maasai, Thornicroft and Angolan are all species of which animal?
6. 'Fidelity Fiduciary Bank' and 'Let's Go Fly a Kite' are songs from which film musical?
7. In which US state is Cape Canaveral?
8. Who was the Prime Minister of Great Britain for the majority of World War Two?
9. What are the six colours on a Rubik's Cube?
10. What does a philatelist collect?
11. David Bowie, whose hits include 'Space Oddity,' and 'Life on Mars,' died 10th January 2016. What was his real name?
12. What was discovered in November 1922 by archaeologist Howard Carter?
13. Which medical service originated in Queensland, Australia in 1928?
14. Which Dutch painter, born in 1606, created approaching one hundred self-portraits?
15. Hanoi is the capital city of which country?

Answers

1. Daffodils 2. The Rivals 3. Idi Amin 4. Blondie 5. Giraffe
6. Mary Poppins 7. Florida 8. Winston Churchill 9. White, yellow, orange, red, green and blue 10. Postage stamps
11. David Jones 12. The tomb of Tutankhamun 13. The Flying Doctors 14. Rembrandt 15. Vietnam

Quiz Forty Two

1. On 25th July 1909, which Frenchman in his Type XI monoplane became the first person to fly across the English Channel?
2. The tiger is native to which continent?
3. In the comic books and feature films Peter Parker is the real name of which superhero?
4. What name is given to the coloured part of the eye?
5. Henry Winkler played the role of The Fonz in which American television sitcom?
6. Which British rock band composed the music for the 1979 film 'Quadrophenia'?
7. 'It is a truth universally acknowledged, that a single man in possession of a good fortune, must be in want of a wife,' are the opening lines of which Jane Austen novel?
8. In computing what is Mb short for?
9. Which city hosted the 1936 Summer Olympics?
10. By what more common name is iron pyrites better known?
11. Alphabetically what is the first country in Africa?
12. What is another word for lexicon?
13. What are the two ingredients of marzipan?
14. A shuttlecock is used in which sport?
15. What is the hardest substance in the human body?

Answers

1. Louis Blériot 2. Asia 3. Spider-Man 4. Iris 5. Happy Days 6. The Who 7. Pride and Prejudice 8. Megabyte 9. Berlin 10. Fool's gold 11. Algeria 12. Dictionary 13. Sugar and almonds 14. Badminton 15.Tooth enamel

Quiz Forty Three

1. A cube has how many sides?
2. The ulna is a long bone in which part of the body?
3. Which ocean lies between Africa and Australia and south of Asia?
4. Who wrote the novel 'Gone with the Wind'?
5. What is the name of the lion in C. S. Lewis's The Chronicles of Narnia series?
6. Alphabetically which state of the USA comes last?
7. The leaves of which plant provide the staple diet of silkworms?
8. Which species of snake has varieties called rock, Indian, ball and reticulated?
9. What is the capital city of Tibet?
10. Which Swedish chemist and engineer invented dynamite?
11. What is the chemical symbol for lead?
12. What does the French word 'Pomme' translate to in English?
13. The term renal refers to what part of the human body?
14. On the television programme 'Sesame Street' who is Ernie's best friend and roommate?
15. Mikrowelle is the German word for which kitchen appliance?

Answers

1. Six 2. Arm 3. Indian Ocean 4. Margaret Mitchell 5. Aslan
6. Wyoming 7. Mulberry 8. Python 9. Lhasa 10. Alfred Nobel
11. Pb 12. Apple 13. Kidneys 14. Bert 15. Microwave

Quiz Forty Four

1. What is the southernmost capital city in the world?
2. What is the term for when the moon passes between the earth and sun, blocking out light from the sin?
3. What does the cartoon character Popeye eat to give him strength?
4. In which game is a squidger used?
5. In Greek mythology which King turned everything he touched to gold?
6. What is the main ingredient of an omelette?
7. How many keys does a modern piano have?
8. Who won the Academy Award for Best Actress in 2009 for her role as Leigh Anne Tuohy in 'The Blind Side'?
9. Which ocean separates Africa and Australia?
10. Which famous male singer had a 2015 hit with 'Stitches'?
11. Shaquille O'Neal is associated with which sport?
12. A gosling is the young of which bird?
13. What is the capital city of the Philippines?
14. A gherkin is a pickled what?
15. What is the name of Sherlock Holmes' landlady?

Answers

1. Wellington 2. Solar eclipse 3. Spinach 4. Tiddlywinks
5. King Midas 6. Egg 7. 88 8. Sandra Bullock 9. Indian Ocean
10. Shawn Mendes 11. Basketball 12. Goose 13. Manila
14. Cucumber 15. Mrs Hudson

Quiz Forty Five

1. Which author's works include 'The Twits' and 'The BFG'?
2. In which English county is the city of Truro?
3. Who was the founder of the Scout Movement?
4. In which part of the human body is the patella located?
5. Which English king had six wives?
6. A chukka is a period of play in which sport?
7. Which historical figure was killed by Hawaiian natives in 1779?
8. A murder is the collective name for which bird?
9. Which actor played the role of Draco Malfoy in the Harry Potter films?
10. Which city was capital of West Germany from 1949 until 1990?
11. Who won the Academy Award for Best Actor in 2007 for his role as Daniel Plainview in 'There Will Be Blood'?
12. Which is the largest of the Great Lakes of North America?
13. Which chess piece can only move diagonally?
14. What is the French word for Tuesday?
15. The world's first skyscraper, the ten-story Home Insurance Building was built in 1884-85, in which US city?

Answers

1. Roald Dahl 2. Cornwall 3. Robert Baden-Powell 4. Knee 5. Henry VIII 6. Polo 7. Captain James Cook 8. Crow 9. Tom Felton 10. Bonn 11. Daniel Day-Lewis 12. Superior 13. Bishop 14. Mardi 15. Chicago

Quiz Forty Six

1. What is the name of Han Solo's spacecraft?
2. Which river flows through Rome?
3. What is the name of Long John Silver's parrot in the novel 'Treasure Island'?
4. At what temperature does water boil on the Fahrenheit scale?
5. Which is the only US state to begin with the letter P?
6. What are words that have the opposite meaning to each other called?
7. In America it is known as a faucet, what do the British call it?
8. On 14th December 1911 which explorer was the first to reach the South Pole?
9. Where in the human body can the substance cerumen be found?
10. Switzerland is divided into twenty-six what?
11. Which actress played the role of as Miss Moneypenny in the James Bond films during the Pierce Brosnan years?
12. What instrument in a road vehicle measures distance travelled?
13. Harris, Lewis and Donegal are all types of which fabric?
14. A tercentenary is an anniversary of how many years?
15. What are the clothes a jockey wears called?

Answers

1. Millennium Falcon 2. Tiber 3. Captain Flint 4. 212 degrees 5. Pennsylvania 6. Antonyms 7. Tap 8. Roald Amundsen 9. The ears 10. Cantons 11. Samantha Bond 12. Odometer 13. Tweed 14. 300 15. Silks

Quiz Forty Seven

1. What is the captain of a yacht customarily called?
2. What the name of the ship that Francis Drake circumnavigated the world from 1577 to 1580, called?
3. Which European capital city was destroyed by an earthquake in November 1755?
4. Which country was until 1825, called Upper Peru?
5. What is the science of correcting deformities of the skeleton?
6. On which 1913 George Bernard Shaw play is the musical 'My Fair Lady' based?
7. Which Academy Award winning actor was born Kevin Fowler in July 1959?
8. What nickname was given to England's controversial 1932 cricket tour of Australia?
9. In motor racing, which flag is waved to show the winner?
10. The Wailing Wall is located in which Middle Eastern city?
11. In the fairy tale, which bird laid golden eggs?
12. What is a male elephant called?
13. In J. K. Rowling's Harry Potter books what was Lord Voldemort's birth name?
14. 'Eine kleine Nachtmusik,' 'The Magic Flute,' and 'Cosi fan Tutte,' are works by which Austrian born composer?
15. What was the currency in Spain before the euro?

Answers

1. Skipper 2. Golden Hind 3. Lisbon 4. Bolivia 5. Orthopaedics 6. Pygmalion 7. Kevin Spacey 8. Bodyline 9. Black and white chequered flag 10. Jerusalem 11. Goose 12. A bull 13. Tom Marvolo Riddle 14. Wolfgang Amadeus Mozart 15. Peseta

Quiz Forty Eight

1. In which country are the holy cities of Mecca and Medina?
2. Which illusionist and stunt performer was born Erich Weisz on 24th March 1874, in Budapest, Hungary?
3. Huey, Dewey, and Louie were the nephews of which cartoon character?
4. 'It was the best of times, it was the worst of times,' are the opening lines of which Charles Dickens' novel?
5. How many players are on each side in a game of rugby league?
6. Which letter represents the number 100 in Roman numerals?
7. The prefix gastro refers to which bodily organ?
8. What breed of farm animal is a Polwarth?
9. Which literary doctor owns a parrot called Polynesia?
10. In which religion is the cow considered to be sacred?
11. Paris international airport is named after which French general and statesman?
12. Which international non-governmental organization founded in 196, has a panda as its emblem?
13. In which country are motorways called Autostrade?
14. From 1999 and 2003 Nasser Hussain captained which international test cricket side?
15. Born on 15th March 1975, how is American rapper, singer/songwriter, musician and DJ William Adams professionally known?

Answers

1. Saudi Arabia 2. Harry Houdini 3. Donald Duck 4. A Tale of Two Cities 5. 13 6. C 7. Stomach 8. Sheep 9. Dr Doolittle 10. Hinduism 11. Charles de Gaulle 12. World Wildlife Fund 13. Italy 14. England 15. will.i.am

Quiz Forty Nine

1. What is the name of the fairy in Peter Pan?
2. Rick Allen plays drums for which English rock band?
3. Which 1995 film, starring Mel Gibson, told the story of William Wallace?
4. Members of which profession take the Hippocratic Oath?
5. The 1726 novel 'Gulliver's Travels' was a work by which Anglo-Irish writer and cleric who became Dean of St Patrick's Cathedral, Dublin?
6. Nelson's Column, built in 1843, is a monument in which London square?
7. Who was British Prime Minister between 1979 and 1990?
8. San Andreas, Vice City, and Liberty City are fictional cities in which video game series?
9. Which river flows through Paris?
10. Which member of the British royal family was born on 15th September 1984?
11. Which American aviator made the first solo transatlantic flight in 1927, in his airplane 'The Spirit of St. Louis'?
12. First performed in 1953 the play 'Waiting for Godot' is a work by which Irish writer?
13. 17th March is which Saint's Day?
14. Kampala is the capital city of which African country?
15. Which tax, relating to buildings, was first applied in England in 1695?

Answers

1. Tinker Bell 2. Def Leppard 3. Braveheart 4. Medical 5. Jonathan Swift 6. Trafalgar 7. Margaret Thatcher 8. Grand Theft Auto 9. The Seine 10. Prince Harry 11. Charles Lindbergh 12. Samuel Beckett 13. St Patrick 14. Uganda 15. Window tax

Quiz Fifty

1. The Kelvin scale is a measure of what?
2. How is Scottish record producer, DJ, singer and songwriter born Adam Richard Wiles on 17th January 1984, known professionally?
3. The role of Finn in the 2015 film ‘Star Wars: The Force Awakens’ was played by which English actor?
4. Atriums and ventricles are parts of which organ of the human body?
5. Since 1848 the Élysée Palace has been the official residence of the holder of which post?
6. Rebecca Rabbit and Suzy Sheep are characters from which children’s television show?
7. A squirrel’s nest is called a what?
8. In Roman mythology, who was the Messenger of the gods?
9. What is the term Sat Nav short for?
10. In 1789 on which island did the mutineers from HMS Bounty settle?
11. In 2015 Justin Trudeau became the 23rd Prime Minister of which country?
12. At 3964 miles, what is the longest river in China?
13. Catriona and Maris Piper are types of which vegetable?
14. The role of Blake Carrington in the television series ‘Dynasty’ was played by which actor?
15. What is the capital city of Cyprus?

Answers

1. Temperature 2. Calvin Harris 3. John Boyega 4. The heart 5. President of France 6. Peppa Pig 7. Drey 8. Mercury 9. Satellite Navigation 10. Pitcairn Island 11. Canada 12. Yangtze 13. Potato 14. John Forsythe 15. Nicosia

Quiz Fifty One

1. What was the name of the boy whose toys came alive in the 'Toy Story' films?
2. What is the name of Ben Affleck's younger brother, who is also an actor?
3. The fictional detective Jules Maigret was created by which Belgian writer?
4. The loganberry is a cross between a raspberry and which other fruit?
5. After who was the Teddy Bear named?
6. 'The Four Seasons,' 'Gloria' and 'Magnificat' are works by which Italian composer?
7. Off the coast of which Australian state is the Great Barrier Reef located?
8. In the nursery rhyme what was Little Miss Muffet eating when the spider came along?
9. Who painted the ceiling of the Sistine Chapel between 1508 and 1512?
10. What is the more common name for the tympanic membrane?
11. Under what name did Agnes Gonxha Bojaxhiu win the 1979 Nobel Peace prize?
12. Columbus sailed to America in three ships, the Santa Maria and which other two?
13. Bucephalus was the horse of which ancient Greek king?
14. 'Blood Father,' 'The Patriot' and 'Payback,' are films starring which actor?
15. What was the area between the opposing trenches known as during the First World War?

Answers

1. Andy Davis 2. Casey 3. Georges Simenon 4. Blackberry
5. US President Theodore Roosevelt 6. Antonio Vivaldi
7. Queensland 8. Curds and whey 9. Michelangelo 10.
Ear drum 11. Mother Teresa 12. Nina and Pinta 13.
Alexander the Great 14. Mel Gibson 15. No Man's Land

Quiz Fifty Two

1. Which sportsman became Marilyn Monroe's second husband in January 1954?
2. What was the name of the Duke of Wellington's horse at the Battle of Waterloo?
3. Who was elected as Prime Minister of Zimbabwe in 1980?
4. Who did John Hinckley attempt to assassinate in 1981?
5. From whom did the US purchase Alaska in 1867?
6. Who in 1986, at the age of 20 years, became the youngest ever heavyweight boxing champion of the World?
7. Dedicated 28th October 1886, which nation gave the Statue of Liberty to the United States?
8. Which female singer released a hit song called 'Wildest Dreams' in 2015?
9. Which performer, who won the Eurovision Song Contest twice, in 1980 and 1987, also composed the winning song in 1992?
10. What is a vein in a rock containing mineral deposits called?
11. What kind of creature was the now extinct dodo?
12. What currency is used in South Africa?
13. Which town in West Bengal gave its name to a high quality tea?
14. Fictional character Diana Prince is the secret identity of which superheroine?
15. What is the name of former US President and First Lady Bill and Hillary Clinton's daughter?

Answers

1. Joe DiMaggio 2. Copenhagen 3. Robert Mugabe
4. President Ronald Reagan 5. Russia 6. Mike Tyson
7. France 8. Taylor Swift 9. Johnny Logan 10. Lode
11. Bird 12. The Rand 13. Darjeeling 14. Wonder Woman
15. Chelsea

Quiz Fifty Three

1. Which actor played the title role in the Crocodile Dundee films?
2. Which two countries are separated by the sea called Kattegat?
3. 'Good Vibrations,' 'California Girls' and 'Surfin' U.S.A.,' were hits for which pop group?
4. Tanganyika and Zanzibar combined in 1964 to form which country?
5. Born in 1874, what nationality was composer Gustav Holst?
6. How many minutes are there in a 24 hours?
7. Which actor played the role of Jakie Rabinowitz in The Jazz Singer, the first feature-length motion picture with synchronized sound?
8. The medieval arbalest was what type of weapon?
9. The Volkswagen Beetle was launched in 1937, who was the designer?
10. Which architect designed the Sagrada Familia in Barcelona?
11. Ras ben Sakka is the most northerly point in Africa, in which country is it?
12. The role of Madison the Mermaid in the 1984 film 'Splash' was played by which actress?
13. What nationality was the surrealist artist René Magritte?
14. According to the song, who went to sea with silver buckles on his knee?
15. With which musical instrument was Belgium-born French jazz musician Jean 'Django' Reinhardt associated?

Answers

1. Paul Hogan 2. Denmark and Sweden 3. Beach Boys
4. Tanzania 5. British 6. 1440 7. Al Jolson
8. Crossbow 9. Ferdinand Porsche 10. Antoni Gaudí
11. Tunisia 12. Daryl Hannah 13. Belgian 14. Bobby
Shafto 15. Guitar

Quiz Fifty Four

1. Which Christmas song, composed by James Lord Pierpont in 1857, was originally titled ‘The One Horse Open Sleigh’?
2. How many stars feature on the flag of New Zealand?
3. Simon Le Bon is the lead singer of which pop group?
4. ‘Blood and Fire’ is the motto of which organisation?
5. What river flows over the Victoria Falls?
6. Valentine and Proteus were the names of the title characters of which Shakespeare play?
7. A Kerry Blue is a breed of which animal?
8. An isobar is the line on a weather map connecting points of equal what?
9. Origami is the art of what?
10. Rosaviakosmos is the Russian counterpart of which US organisation?
11. What is the name of the clockwork device used by musicians to measure time?
12. In 1991 Edith Cresson became the first female Prime Minister of which European country?
13. Reginald Dwight is the birth name of which singer/songwriter?
14. Fruit, pipistrelle and horseshoe are all types of what creature?
15. Who provides the voice of the Princess Fiona in the film ‘Shrek’?

Answers

1. Jingle Bells 2. Four 3. Duran Duran 4. The Salvation Army 5. Zambezi 6. The Two Gentlemen of Verona 7. Dog 8. Pressure 9. Paper folding 10. NASA 11. Metronome 12. France 13. Elton John 14. Bat 15. Cameron Diaz

Quiz Fifty Five

1. Leslie Charteris wrote which series of books featuring the character Simon Templar?
2. What name is given to the number on the bottom of a fraction?
3. Who, in 1842, composed 'The Wedding March'?
4. What is the name of the longest river in Italy?
5. Who won the Academy Award for Best Actor in 2008 for his role as Harvey Milk in 'Milk'?
6. Who was fatally wounded by John Wilkes Booth in 1865 whilst watching the play Our American Cousin?
7. What is the chief ingredient of the Russian soup solyanka?
8. 'Listen to the ground, there is music all around' are lyrics from which Bee Gees song?
9. Actress Linda Carter played which superheroine in a 1970s television series?
10. What is the capital city of the US state of New York?
11. The city of Marrakesh is located in which country?
12. What did Abel Tasman call Tasmania when he discovered it in November 1642?
13. Walter Mondale served as US vice-president to whom?
14. Justin Timberlake was a vocalist with which band?
15. What was the first name of Yale, inventor of the cylinder lock?

Answers

1. The Saint 2. Denominator 3. Felix Mendelssohn 4. Po 5. Sean Penn 6. Abraham Lincoln 7. Cucumber 8. Night Fever 9. Wonder Woman 10. Albany 11. Morocco 12. Van Diemen's Land 1 3. Jimmy Carter 14. *NSYNC 15. Linus

Quiz Fifty Six

1. What was the nationality of the female climber, who on 16th May 1975 became the first woman to reach the summit of Mount Everest?
2. What was the name of the character played by Bruce Willis is the 'Die Hard' series of films?
3. Which John Steinbeck novel tells the story of George Milton and Lennie Small?
4. Which Norwegian politician was the first Secretary General of the United Nations?
5. Jakarta is the capital city of which Southeast Asian nation?
6. Cd is an abbreviation for which unit of luminous intensity?
7. In the animated television series who voices the character of Bart Simpson?
8. Which supermodel is nicknamed The Body?
9. Jasmine and long grain are both varieties of what food?
10. Ayer's Rock is a landmark in which Australian state?
11. Which series of sci-fi films features a hovercraft called the Nebuchadnezzar?
12. Java, Columbian and Kenyan are all types of what beverage?
13. What does the AA stand for in the name of the author AA Milne?
14. How many hearts does an octopus have?
15. Which French tennis star, born in 1904, was nicknamed The Crocodile?

Answers

1. Japanese 2. John McClane 3. Of Mice and Men 4. Trygve Lie 5. Indonesia 6. Candela 7. Nancy Cartwright 8. Elle Macpherson 9. Rice 10. Northern Territory 11. The Matrix 12. Coffee 13. Alan Alexander 14. Three 15. René Lacoste

Quiz Fifty Seven

1. What type of triangle has three sides of differing length?
2. Which outlaw was portrayed by Mick Jagger in a 1969 film and by Heath Ledger in a 2003 film?
3. What name was given to the Supreme Court of ancient Rome?
4. In the human body what is the name of the white area at the base of a fingernail?
5. Which physicist and chemist invented the vacuum flask in 1892?
6. Laszlo Biro, inventor of the modern ballpoint pen was born 29th September 1899 in which country?
7. What animal is the symbol of the motor manufacturer Suzuki?
8. Acht is the German word for which number?
9. What is etymology the study of?
10. What is the official language of Mexico?
11. What does the abbreviation AKA stand for?
12. Which male singer had a hit song with 'Thinking Out Loud' in 2014?
13. The winner of which sporting event is awarded the Venus Rosewater Dish?
14. Which famous figure was released from imprisonment on 11th February 1990?
15. Posh, Scary, Sporty, Ginger and Baby were known collectively as which pop group?

Answers

1. Scalene 2. Ned Kelly 3. The Senate 4. Lunula 5. James Dewar 6. Hungary 7. Rhinoceros 8. Eight 9. Words 10. Spanish 11. Also known as 12. Ed Sheeran 13. Ladies Wimbledon singles championship 14. Nelson Mandela 15. Spice Girls

Quiz Fifty Eight

1. 'Slowhand' is the nickname of which musician?
2. Which of the Great Lakes is entirely located within the United States of America?
3. Capitoline Hill is the tallest hill in which city?
4. How many lines does a sonnet contain?
5. What were the names of the two rival gangs in 'West Side Story'?
6. On the 14th day of which month do the French celebrate Bastille Day?
7. The Boxer Rebellion took place between 1899 and 1901 in which country?
8. What language did Polish born doctor L. L. Zamenhof devise?
9. 'Red Vineyard' was the title of the only painting that which artist sold during his lifetime?
10. In Moscow, what is known as 'the city within a city'?
11. Which 1945 novel features a horse called Boxer?
12. In an Italian restaurant, what are grissini?
13. The role of Sally Albright in the 1989 film 'When Harry Met Sally...,' was played by which actress?
14. What is the name of the novel, published in 2015, written by Harper Lee as a sequel to 'To Kill A Mockingbird'?
15. How many players comprise a netball team?

Answers

1. Eric Clapton 2. Michigan 3. Rome 4. 14 5. Jets and Sharks 6. July 7. China 8. Esperanto 9. Vincent Van Gogh 10. The Kremlin 11. Animal Farm 12. Breadsticks 13. Meg Ryan 14. Go Set A Watchman 15. 7

Quiz Fifty Nine

1. What is the name of the recording company founded by The Beatles in 1968?
2. Which planet is named after the Roman goddess of love and beauty?
3. Who wrote the poem 'Paradise Lost'?
4. Blanche DuBois and Stella Kowalski are characters in which Tennessee Williams' play?
5. Who wrote the novel 'Chitty, Chitty, Bang, Bang'?
6. The airline QANTAS is based in which country?
7. What is fermented to produce the drink mead?
8. What is the capital city of Canada?
9. Elephant, fur and crabeater are all species of which animal?
10. How is 1600 Pennsylvania Avenue better known?
11. In the human body what is the more common name for renal calculi?
12. What were first classified by the Galton-Henry system in 1901?
13. Alphabetically what is the last chemical element?
14. Which aircraft company makes the Jumbo jet?
15. Which professional footballer, who died in 1993, was captain of West Ham United for more than ten years and captain of the England team that won the 1966 World Cup?

Answers

1. Apple Records 2. Venus 3. John Milton 4. A Streetcar named Desire 5. Ian Fleming 6. Australia 7. Honey 8. Ottawa 9. Seal 10. The White House 11. Kidney stones 12. Fingerprints 13. Zirconium 14. Boeing 15. Bobby Moore

Quiz Sixty

1. Which Australian born actor played James Bond in the 1969 'On Her Majesty's Secret Service?'
2. What does the E stand for in food additives known as E numbers?
3. The orchestral interlude 'Flight of the Bumblebee' was written by which Russian composer?
4. Which collection of tales from a Greek story teller includes 'The Tortoise and the Hare'?
5. Issur Danielovitch is the real name of which veteran actor, whose films include 'Lust for Life' and 'Tough Guys'?
6. Which European country was ruled by Francisco Franco between 1939 and 1975?
7. What word was the name given to the feudal code of the Japanese Samurai?
8. Paul McCartney and Wings sang the theme song on which James Bond film?
9. The CN Tower is located in which North American city?
10. What is the name of the brother of Sherlock Holmes?
11. Who created the fictional character of Walter Mitty?
12. The Circuit Gilles Villeneuve is a motor racing circuit is in which country?
13. Which 1860s novel opens with the line, 'Christmas wouldn't be Christmas without any presents'?
14. STR is the airport code of which European city?
15. What word is the collective name for a group of monkeys?

Answers

1. George Lazenby 2. Europe 3. Nikolai Rimsky-Korsakov 4. Aesop's Fables 5. Kirk Douglas 6. Spain 7. Bushido 8. Live and Let Die 9. Toronto 10. Mycroft 11. James Thurber 12. Canada 13. Little Women 14. Stuttgart 15. Troop

Quiz Sixty One

1. Which English sculptor, born in 1898, created rounded forms such as 'Reclining Figure'?
2. Geena Davis and Susan Sarandon played the title roles in which 1991 film?
3. Who wrote the novel 'Silence of the Lambs'?
4. Which fish does caviar come from?
5. Which country was invaded by Germany on 1st September 1939?
6. A bite from what is said to have killed Cleopatra?
7. Which country was once called Rhodesia?
8. Which Justin Bieber song begins with the lyrics 'You gotta go and get angry at all of my honesty'?
9. What is the official language of Austria?
10. Which herb is used to make Pesto?
11. Which pop band was fronted by Freddie Mercury?
12. Football team Benfica come from which country?
13. What were the names of the five D-Day beaches?
14. Prior to 1825 in which city were French kings crowned?
15. Where in the human body are the metatarsal arches located?

Answers

1. Henry Moore 2. Thelma and Louise 3. Thomas Harris 4. Sturgeon 5. Poland 6. Asp 7. Zimbabwe 8. Sorry 9. German 10. Basil 11. Queen 12. Portugal 13. Gold, Juno, Sword , Utah and Omaha 14. heims 15. Feet

Quiz Sixty Two

1. Which two states fought the Punic Wars, a series of three wars fought from 264 BC to 146 BC?
2. Which iconic building was Danish architect Jørn Utzon most notable for designing?
3. ‘Revolver,’ ‘Rubber Soul’ and ‘Let It Be’ were album releases by which band?
4. To which actress was British actor Michael Wilding married from 1952 until 1957?
5. Which actress played the role of Vivian Ward in the 1990 romantic comedy ‘Pretty Woman’?
6. In which US State is the skiing resort of Aspen?
7. Which Italian driver won the first official Formula One World Champion in 1950?
8. What name is given to a male guinea pig?
9. Which mountain range is known as The Backbone of Italy?
10. Which 1939 film featured the song ‘Ding Dong the Witch Is Dead’?
11. Which Asian country is known as the ‘Land of Smiles’?
12. According to the Noël Coward song who ‘go out in the midday sun’?
13. Which American track and field athlete won four gold medals at the 1936 Berlin Olympics?
14. What were the surnames of US television cartoonists William and Joseph, whose creations include Yogi Bear?
15. Which SI unit measures loudness?

Answers

1. Rome and Carthage 2. The Sydney Opera House 3. The Beatles 4. Elizabeth Taylor 5. Julia Roberts 6. Colorado 7. Giuseppe Farina 8. Boar 9. Apennines 10. The Wizard of Oz 11. Thailand 12. Mad dogs and Englishmen 13. Jesse Owens 14. Hanna and Barbera 15. Decibel

Quiz Sixty Three

1. What is the capital city of the Australian island state of Tasmania?
2. Which German composer wrote the opera The Flying Dutchman?
3. The song 'Nessum Dorma' features in which opera?
4. What was the name of the character played by Michael Caine in the 1965 British espionage film 'The Ipcress File'?
5. Which actress is the mother of the actress Kate Hudson?
6. In which New York borough is Wall Street located?
7. With which country does Holland form a 450 km (280 miles) border?
8. Which actress did Prince Rainier of Monaco marry in 1956?
9. What type of creature is a flying fox?
10. By what name was Francois Duvalier, the President of Haiti from 1957 to 1971 also known?
11. In the NATO alphabet what three words represent the letters X, Y, Z?
12. Electric power is typically measured in which units?
13. What is the centre of an atom called?
14. In relation to mobile phones what is the area covered by a base station called?
15. Which English Romanic poet drowned on 8th July 1822, at the age of 29, in a storm off the coast of Italy?

Answers

1. Hobart 2. Richard Wagner 3. Turandot 4. Harry Palmer
5. Goldie Hawn 6. Manhattan 7. Belgium 8. Grace Kelly
9. Bat 10. Papa Doc 11. X Ray, Yankee, Zulu 12. Watts
13. Nucleus 14. Cell 15. Percy Bysshe Shelley

Quiz Sixty Four

1. What does the French term ‘plat du jour’ mean on a restaurant menu?
2. What is the waxy substance obtained from sheep called?
3. Which German born playwright and poet wrote ‘The Threepenny Opera’?
4. In November of which year did the Berlin Wall fall?
5. What was the real first name of the 18th century landscape gardener known as ‘Capability’ Brown?
6. Who sang Ireland’s 1970 Eurovision Song Contest winning entry, ‘All Kinds of Everything’?
7. Which role did Tommy Lee Jones play in the 1995 film ‘Batman Forever’?
8. Who wrote the 2003 novel ‘The Da Vinci Code’?
9. ‘Can the Can’ and ‘48 Crash’ were hits for which female singer and bass player?
10. Which English engineer invented the jet engine?
11. Which former world heavyweight champion boxer was nicknamed The Manassa Mauler?
12. The 1859 ‘On The Origin of Species’ was a work by which English naturalist, geologist and biologist?
13. What is the capital city of Hong Kong?
14. Which pair of Disney dogs shared a plate of spaghetti in a 1955 animated film?
15. In the human body what are the four main types of blood groups?

Answers

1. Dish of the day 2. Lanolin 3. Bertolt Brecht 4. 1989 5. Lancelot 6. Dana 7. Harvey Two Face 8. Dan Brown 9. Suzi Quatro 10. Sir Frank Whittle 11. Jack Dempsey 12. Charles Darwin 13. Victoria 14. Lady and the Tramp 15. A, B, AB and O

Quiz Sixty Five

1. Which actor starred opposite Cybill Shepherd in the television series Moonlighting?
2. 'Paul Revere's Ride' and 'The Song of Hiawatha' are works by which American poet, born in 1807?
3. In the film 'Notting Hill' what type of shop did Hugh Grant's character William Thacker own?
4. Suva is the capital and largest city of which South Pacific island?
5. What title did Charlemagne, already king of the Franks, acquire in 800 AD?
6. Which pantomime character is the son of Widow Twankey?
7. What were the first names of the comic opera writers Gilbert and Sullivan?
8. What is the term given to the study of the weather?
9. In T. S. Eliot's 'Old Possum's Book of Practical Cats' what was the name of the The Railway Cat?
10. What is the name of the warm ocean current that flows across the Atlantic?
11. What is the main constituent of natural gas?
12. If the left hand page of a book is called verso, what is the right hand page called?
13. Which actor, who played the role of Napoleon Solo in the 1960s television series 'The Man from U.N.C.L.E.,' died on 11th November 2016?
14. In which 1982 film did Richard Gere play the character Zack Mayo?
15. During World War Two how was the prison camp Oflag IV-C better known?

Answers

1. Bruce Willis 2 Henry Wadsworth Longfellow 3. Book shop 4. Fiji 5. Holy Roman Emperor 6. Aladdin 7. William and Arthur 8. Meteorology 9. Skimbleshanks 10. Gulf Stream 11. Methane 12. Recto 13. Robert Vaughn 14. Officer and a Gentleman 15. Colditz

Quiz Sixty Six

1. Celie is the name of the central character in which 1982 Alice Walker novel?
2. Which late actor played the role of Seymour ‘Sy’ Parrish in the 2002 film ‘One Hour Photo’?
3. In which capital city was the Nobel Prize winner Marie Curie born?
4. Which actress played the role of Daisy Duke in television series ‘The Dukes of Hazzard’?
5. Which unit of measurement is equivalent to 4,840 sq yards?
6. During which war was the television series ‘Band of Brothers’ set?
7. Which country was ruled by the Romanov dynasty from 1613 to 1917?
8. What is the ancient Chinese art of placement called?
9. In medicine what is examined by an otoscope?
10. The US First Lady from 1981-89, died 6th March 2016. Who was she?
11. Which part of the USA is often referred to as Tinseltown?
12. What animal is often described as laughing?
13. Common Blue, Orange Tip and Painted Lady are all the names of what?
14. What was New York City called before 1664?
15. Which 2015 Little Mix song features Jason Derulo?

Answers

1. The Color Purple 2. Robin Williams 3. Warsaw 4. Catherine Bach 5. Acre 6. World War Two 7. Russia 8. Feng shui 9. The ear 10. Nancy Reagan 11. Hollywood 12. Hyena 13. Butterflies 14. New Amsterdam 15. Secret Love Song

Quiz Sixty Seven

1. Which actress received an Academy Award nomination for her role in the 1995 'The Bridges of Madison County'?
2. In Indian cookery which vegetable is called Aloo?
3. In the human body what common name is given to the sternum?
4. What someone wearing crampons be doing?
5. In the human body which muscles are located in the thigh?
6. Who exchanged faces with John Travolta in the 1997 film 'Face/Off'?
7. The Battle of Little Big Horn took place in which US state?
8. 'Down the Rabbit Hole' is the opening chapter of which children's novel?
9. Which city is the capital of Sweden?
10. 'The Dark Side of the Moon' and 'Wish You Were Here' are albums by which English band?
11. The Formula One Marina Bay Street Circuit is in which Asian country?
12. On an analogue clock face, which number lies opposite 5?
13. Which flower shares its name with a mythological character that rejected the love of Echo?
14. Until 1867 what title was given to the military leaders of Japan?
15. What is the name of the mythological three-headed dog that guards the entrance to Hades?

Answers

1. Meryl Streep 2. Potato 3. Breastbone 4. Climbing 5. Quadriceps 6. Nicolas Cage 7. Montana. 8. Alice's Adventures in Wonderland 9. Stockholm 10. Pink Floyd 11. Singapore 12. 11 13. Narcissus 14. Shogun 15. Cerberus

Quiz Sixty Eight

1. England's national rugby union side play their home games at which ground?
2. Minus 40 degrees Celsius is equal to how many degrees Fahrenheit?
3. Haiku is a form of poetry that originated in what country?
4. What instrument used in aircraft to measure height above sea level?
5. What James Bond film title is also a species of duck?
6. What blood group abbreviated to Rh is named after a species of monkey?
7. How is funambulism more commonly known?
8. What is the medical name for the skull?
9. Courgettes and pumpkins both belong to which plant family?
10. What is the 10th letter of the Greek alphabet?
11. Born in Bonn, Germany in 1770, what was the first name of composer Beethoven?
12. Painted in two phases in the 1880s, what is the subject of Pierre-Auguste Renoir's work 'Les Parapluies'?
13. Which Academy Award winning 1990 film featured the characters of Chief Ten Bears and Kicking Bird?
14. Which textile is made from the fibres of the Flax plant?
15. Which river forms the boundary between the USA and Mexico?

Answers

1. Twickenham 2. Minus 40 F 3. Japan 4. Altimeter
5. Goldeneye 6. Rhesus 7. Tightrope walking 8. Cranium
9. Marrow 10. Kappa 11. Ludwig 12. Umbrellas
13. Dances with Wolves 14. Linen 15. Rio Grande

Quiz Sixty Nine

1. In what sport do players take long and short corners?
2. 'Little Red Rooster' was a 1964 No 1 for which band?
3. Tinie Tempah's hit song 'Not Letting Go', featured which female artist?
4. Saigon was the previous name of which city?
5. Poseidon is the Greek god of what?
6. Which vitamin is known as Ascorbic Acid?
7. Dutch, French and which other are the official languages of Belgium?
8. What is the world's longest mountain range?
9. In which 1960s television series did the character Little Joe Cartwright appear?
10. Which Shakespeare play features a wizard called Prospero?
11. What type of pasta is named after the Italian for small tongues?
12. Olfactory refers to which of the body's senses?
13. On which part of the bagpipes is the melody played?
14. Sardines are the young of which fish?
15. In what sport is the Fosbury flop technique used?

Answers

1. Hockey 2. The Rolling Stones 3. Jess Glynne 4. Ho Chi Minh 5. The sea 6. Vitamin C 7. German 8. Andes 9. Bonanza 10. The Tempest 11. Linguini 12. Smell 13. Chanter 14. Pilchard 15. High jump

Quiz Seventy

1. Red fronted and ring tailed are both species of which animal?
2. Which world leader resigned on Christmas Day 1991?
3. What is the most sacred river to Hindus?
4. What is the nickname of Beethoven's 'Symphony No. 3'?
5. Which mountain range extends through Morocco, Algeria and Tunisia?
6. What was the name of the first man made satellite to orbit the Earth, launched on 4th October 1957 by the Soviet Union?
7. Which 1818 gothic horror novel was written by Mary Shelley?
8. If canine equates to dog, what word equates to bear?
9. Which thoroughfare in New York City is nicknamed 'The Great White Way'?
10. Which actor played the title role in the 1990 romantic dark fantasy film 'Edward Scissorhands'?
11. What does the word 'sekt' signify on a German wine bottle label?
12. What name is given to a watercraft with two hulls?
13. Which English physicist wrote the 1988 book 'A Brief History of Time'?
14. NB is the zip code of which US state?
15. Which hormone stimulates the nervous system and raises the heart rate?

Answers

1. Lemur 2. Mikhail Gorbachev 3. Ganges 4. Eroica
5. Atlas 6. Sputnik 1 7. Frankenstein 8. Ursine
9. Broadway 10.Johnny Depp 11. Sparkling
12. Catamaran 13. Stephen Hawking 14. Nebraska
15. Adrenalin

Quiz Seventy One

1. Brisbane is the capital and most populous city of which Australian state?
2. Phobos and Deimos are the two moons of which planet?
3. Who wrote the novel 'The Thorn Birds'?
4. Who sang the theme song to the 1974 James Bond film 'The Man with the Golden Gun'?
5. Which rap star played the role of Huggy Bear in the 2003 film 'Starsky and Hutch'?
6. How many stars does the flag of the USA have?
7. On a QWERTY computer keyboard which letter is between G and J?
8. Which author, born in 1892, had the middle names of Ronald Reuel?
9. If the Orient means the East, what word means the West?
10. What is the name of the award presented for the best film at the Berlin International Film Festival?
11. Which city is overlooked by Table Mountain?
12. Which is the principal island of Japan?
13. Which actor played the role of US President James Marshall in the 1997 film 'Air Force One'?
14. Roquefort is made from the milk of which animal?
15. In medicine, gingivitis is inflammation of what parts of the body?

Answers

1. Queensland 2. Mars 3. Colleen McCullough
4. Lulu 5. Snoop Doggy Dogg 6. 50 7. H 8. JRR
Tolkien 9. Occident 10. The Golden Bear 11. Cape
Town 12. Honshu 13. Harrison Ford 14. Sheep
15. Gums

Quiz Seventy Two

1. Which Australian city stands on the River Yarra?
2. Into which ocean does the Amazon empty?
3. What is the only species of venomous snake native to the United Kingdom?
4. Which American author wrote the novels ‘The Call of the Wild’ and ‘White Fang’?
5. Who wrote the 1842 poem The Pied Piper of Hamelin?
6. Which bird proclaimed, ‘Nevermore’ in the 1845 narrative poem by Edgar Allan Poe?
7. Who provides the voice of the title character in the Shrek films?
8. Which unit of measurement is derived from the Arabic word for seed?
9. What name is given to the indentations on a golf ball?
10. Which gladiator and slave was played by Kirk Douglas in a 1960 classic movie?
11. What is a number called which is divisible only by itself and one?
12. What was the name of the world’s first jet airliner that first carried paying passengers in 1952?
13. Which cartoon character led the gang whose members included Benny the Ball and Choo Choo?
14. Which actor played the role of President Josiah Bartlet in the television drama ‘The West Wing’?
15. What word is the unit measurement for the brightness of stars?

Answers

1. Melbourne 2. Atlantic Ocean 3. Adder 4. Jack London
5. Robert Browning 6. Raven 7. Mike Myers 8. Carat
9. Dimples 10. Spartacus 11. Prime number 12. Comet
13. Top Cat 14. Martin Sheen 15. Magnitude

Quiz Seventy Three

1. What are tiny cracks in the glaze of pottery called?
2. The largest tendon in the body is named after which Greek hero?
3. The Golden Gate Bridge spans which bay?
4. Maurice Micklewhite is the birth name of which English actor?
5. In which 1969 film did Clint Eastwood sing, 'I Talk to the Trees'?
6. Who composed the 1840 German-language opera 'The Flying Dutchman,' about a legendary ghost ship that can never make port and is doomed to sail the oceans forever?
7. Which country is connected to Pakistan by the Khyber Pass?
8. In The Lord of the Rings what is the name of Gandalf's horse?
9. On which island are the majority of the world's lemurs to be found?
10. What name is given to the shadow of the Earth on the moon?
11. A sextant is used to measure what?
12. Which group had a 1967 hit with 'Last Train to Clarkesville'?
13. Which species of whale is the largest creature in the world?
14. William Tell is a legendary hero in which country?
15. What collective name is given to the first ten amendments of the American Constitution?

Answers

1. Crackle 2. Achilles 3. San Francisco Bay 4. Michael Caine 5. Paint Your Wagon 6. Richard Wagner 7. Afghanistan 8. Shadowfax 9. Madagascar 10. Umbra 11. Latitude 12. The Monkees 13. Blue whale 14. Switzerland 15. Bill Of Rights

Quiz Seventy Four

1. In golf, what is meant by the term birdie?
2. Which country does the singer Rihanna come from?
3. Which actor played the title role in the television series 'Dexter'?
4. Which car company manufactured a model called the Silver Ghost?
5. What was the surname of the French brothers, Joseph and Jacques, who were pioneer developers of the hot-air balloon?
6. On television who lived at 1313 Mockingbird Lane, Mockingbird Heights, California?
7. The 1985 'A View to a Kill' was the last James Bond film for which actor?
8. In April 1968 in which city was Martin Luther King assassinated?
9. Het Wilhelmus is the title of the national anthem of which European nation?
10. Which Hollywood actress has the British title of Lady Haden-Guest?
11. What name did Leningrad revert to in 1991?
12. Gillyflower, Honeycrisp and Northern Spy are varieties of which fruit?
13. What nut is used to make satay sauce?
14. What collective name is given to the eight oldest universities in the USA?
15. In May 1932 who became the first female pilot to fly solo across the Atlantic?

Answers

1. One under par 2. Barbados 3. Michael C. Hall 4. Rolls Royce 5. Montgolfier 6. The Munsters 7. Roger Moore 8. Memphis 9. Netherlands 10. Jamie Lee Curtis 11. St Petersburg 12. Apple 13. Peanut 14. The Ivy League 15. Amelia Earhart

Quiz Seventy Five

1. Which major city is found at the mouth of the River Nile?
2. In food what dessert is made from the starch extracted from the pith of a palm tree?
3. 'Never Say Never Again' was a remake of which earlier James Bond film?
4. In the human body what is the more common name for the trachea?
5. Ganymede is a moon which orbits which planet?
6. What is the official language of Cuba?
7. In which year did Russian cosmonaut Valentina Tereshkova become the first woman in space?
8. What does a meteorologist study?
9. Hairy nosed and Queensland are both varieties of which animal?
10. Which word of German origin literally means 'noisy ghost'?
11. Who in 1879 founded the religion of Christian Science?
12. Which country makes Gorgonzola cheese?
13. In 1973 General Pinochet led a military coup in which country?
14. Which Georges Bizet opera heroine worked as a cigarette factory employee?
15. Xander Harris was a fictional character in which fantasy television series that ran from 1997 to 2003?

Answers

1. Alexandria 2. Sago 3. Thunderball 4. Windpipe
5. Jupiter 6. Spanish 7. 1963 8. Weather 9. Wombat
10. Poltergeist 11. Mary Baker Eddy 12. Italy 13. Chile
14. Carmen 15. Buffy the Vampire Slayer

Quiz Seventy Six

1. Which country is surrounded by Belgium, France and Germany?
2. What name is given to the science of attempting to turn base metals into gold?
3. What was the name of the canine partner of Tom Hanks in a 1989 film?
4. Whose assassination on 28th June 1914 precipitated the outbreak of the First World War?
5. Which actor played the role of Charlie Allnut in the 1951 film 'The African Queen'?
6. Which South American city has a name that translates into English as 'River of January'?
7. What word is the name given to the text of an opera?
8. Which Japanese garment has a name that literally means 'thing to wear'?
9. Who designed the uniform of the Swiss Guard, the bodyguards of the Pope?
10. What is Bruce Wayne's secret identity?
11. Which early Renaissance Italian painter's works include 'The Birth of Venus,' and 'Adoration of the Magi'?
12. What vegetable is served with the dish egg florentine?
13. Porsche, the designer of the Volkswagen Beetle had what first name?
14. 'Whatever You Want' and 'Down Down' were hits for which English rock band?
15. The Four Noble Truths are central to which religion?

Answers

1. Luxembourg 2. Alchemy 3. Hooch 4. Archduke
Franz Ferdinand 5. Humphrey Bogart 6. Rio de
Janeiro 7. Libretto 8. Kimono 9. Michelangelo
10. Batman 11. Sandro Botticelli 12. Spinach
13. Ferdinand 14. Status Quo 15. Buddhism

Quiz Seventy Seven

1. In which 1953 film did Marilyn Monroe sing 'Diamonds Are A Girls Best Friend'?
2. What is the medical term for short sightedness?
3. In which 1988 film did Bob Hoskins play a detective called Eddie Valiant? Who Framed
4. Which Australian mammal lays eggs?
5. In golf, what is a hole completed in one under par called?
6. What nationality is Nick Jonas?
7. What are non-precious metals called?
8. What is the capital city of Cuba?
9. Which race was named after a battle fought in 490 BC?
10. With an elevation of 3,640 m (11,942 ft), what is the world's highest capital city?
11. Which French naval officer, explorer and scientist, the co-inventor of the aqualung, sailed in a research ship called The Calypso?
12. What name is given to the science of projectiles?
13. The stiletto heel takes its name from what?
14. William Cody was the real name of which American scout and showman?
15. How is the Alaskan malamute more commonly known?

Answers

1. Gentlemen Prefer Blondes 2. Myopia 3. Roger Rabbit
4. Duck-billed platypus 5. Birdie 6. American 7. Base metals
8. Havana 9. Marathon 10. La Paz 11. Jacques Cousteau
12. Ballistics 13. A dagger 14. Buffalo Bill 15. Husky

Quiz Seventy Eight

1. Actor Peter Falk played the title role in which television detective series?
2. In which European country is the city of Bruges?
3. The Calcutta Cup is a trophy competed for in which sport?
4. What name is given to a young hedgehog?
5. What is the name of the Roman god of beginnings?
6. Which two US states begin with the letter K?
7. What was the name of the German Parliament building that was burnt to the ground in 1933?
8. What was the surname of Chuck, who in 1947 became the first pilot to break the sound barrier?
9. What name is given to the curdled milk from a cow's stomach?
10. 'Call me Ishmael' are the first words of which novel?
11. One imperial tablespoon equals how many teaspoons?
12. Vanessa Mae is famous for playing which musical instrument?
13. In the title of a Chekov play who were Irina, Masha and Olga?
14. What is the only clockwise-rotating planet?
15. The Persistence of Memory was a 1931 painting by which Spanish artist?

Answers

1. Columbo 2. Belgium 3. Rugby Union 4. Hoglet
5. Janus 6. Kansas and Kentucky 7. Reichstag
8. Yeager 9. Rennet 10. Moby Dick 11. Three
12. Violin 13. The Three Sisters 14. Venus
15. Salvador Dalí

Quiz Seventy Nine

1. 'You'll Never Walk Alone' is a song from which Richard Rodgers and Oscar Hammerstein 1945 musical?
2. Which actress played the role of Muriel in the 1994 Australian film 'Muriel's Wedding'?
3. The French town of Dijon is famous for the manufacture of what?
4. What are the two official languages of Finland?
5. What type of cloud produces rain?
6. What is a group of eight musicians called?
7. In 1893 which became the first country in the world to give women the vote?
8. Which metal is the lightest known solid element?
9. Which king of France, who ruled from 1643 until his death in 1715, was known as 'the Sun King'?
10. What is the SI Unit for pressure?
11. Val Kilmer, George Clooney and Christian Bale have all played which character on film?
12. How many degrees do the interior angles of a triangle always equal?
13. What is paint applied to in a fresco?
14. Which English band took its name from a fictional doctor in the film 'Barbarella'?
15. In trivial pursuit, which colour identifies questions on history?

Answers

1. Carousel 2. Toni Collette 3. Mustard 4. Finnish and Swedish 5. Nimbus 6. Octet 7. New Zealand 8. Lithium 9. Louis XIV 10. Pascal 11. Batman 12. 180 degrees 13. Wet plaster 14. Duran Duran 15. Yellow

Quiz Eighty

1. Which politician, who died on 13th August 2016, was President of Cuba from 1976 to 2008?
2. What is the common name for decompression sickness?
3. Trudie Styler married which English musician, singer, songwriter and actor in 1992?
4. What is the name of the hooked staff carried by a bishop as a symbol of pastoral office?
5. What is the name of Shirley MacLaine's actor brother?
6. Which vitamin has the chemical name of retinol?
7. After how many years of marriage is a ruby wedding celebrated?
8. Actress Honor Blackman appeared in which James Bond film?
9. Alphabetically what is the last sign of the zodiac?
10. What is the name for a two-legged animal?
11. What plant does the Colorado beetle attack?
12. Which sport combines cross-country skiing and rifle marksmanship?
13. What does the computer acronym USB stand for?
14. What is the name of the cathedral in Red Square, Moscow?
15. Born in 1832, Charles Lutwidge Dodgson was the real name of which author?

Answers

1. Fidel Castro 2. Bends 3. Sting 4. Crozier 5. Warren Beatty 6. Vitamin A 7. 40 8. Goldfinger 9. Virgo 10. Biped 11. Potato 12. Biathlon 13. Universal Serial Bus 14. St. Basil's 15. Lewis Carroll

Quiz Eighty One

1. In which country is Mount Eiger located?
2. Who played the leading lady in the 1963 Alfred Hitchcock film adaptation of The Birds?
3. In which Australian state is Adelaide?
4. Who was US President at the time of the first moon landing?
5. Who, at the age of 17 in 1985, was the first unseeded man to win the Wimbledon Singles title?
6. Which is the most common element on Earth?
7. Named after its German physicist co-inventor, what goes a Geiger counter measure?
8. Which great ape is found solely in the rainforests of Borneo and Sumatra?
9. Which American artist painted the 1962 Campbell's Soup Tins?
10. What is the technical name for laughing gas?
11. From which plant is Linseed Oil obtained?
12. What is the more common name for the wood hyacinth?
13. Which animal's name is also a type of shoe?
14. In which European country is Dalmatia, from where the Dalmatian dog gets its name?
15. Actress Barbara Bach married which member of The Beatles in 1981?

Answers

1. Switzerland 2. Tippi Hedren 3. Southern Australia
4. Richard Nixon 5. Boris Becker 6. Oxygen
7. Radioactivity 8. Orangutan 9. Andy Warhol
10. Nitrous Oxide 11. Flax 12. Bluebell 13. Mule
14. Croatia 15. Ringo Starr

Quiz Eighty Two

1. What is the name of pirate Johnny Depp plays in the Pirates of the Caribbean film series?
2. Who was the artist of the painting of a farmer with a pitchfork and his daughter, known as 'American Gothic'?
3. How many Russian cosmonauts have walked on the moon?
4. What is the name of the sacred river in the poem 'Kubla Khan'?
5. Who in 1987, together with Per Lindstrand made the first successful transatlantic crossing in a hot-air balloon?
6. Holden Caulfield is the main character in which novel?
7. The greengage is a type of what?
8. Calligraphy is the art of producing decorative what?
9. Alberta and Manitoba are provinces in which country?
10. In Norse mythology what was the name of Odin's eight-legged horse?
11. Which group was once known as The Quarrymen?
12. A potoo is what type of creature?
13. Who was the first Norman King of England, reigning from 1066 until his death in 1087?
14. Which actress played the title role in the television series 'Dr. Quinn, Medicine Woman'?
15. How many figures are there in a completed classic Sudoku puzzle?

Answers

1. Jack Sparrow 2. Grant Wood 3. None 4. Alph
5. Richard Branson 6. The Catcher in the Rye 7. Plum
8. Handwriting 9. Canada 10. Sleipnir 11. The Beatles
12 Bird 13. William the Conqueror 14. Jane Seymour
15. Nine

Quiz Eighty Three

1. Who did Muhammad Ali defeat in the 'Thrilla in Manilla,' which took place 1st October 1975?
2. What name is given to food prepared according to Muslim law?
3. In which European city is the Bosphorus Bridge located?
4. What does a plum become when it is dried?
5. What do dog breeders call a cross between a Labrador and a Poodle?
6. Edam cheese is traditionally covered with what colour wax?
7. What nickname is often given to people with the surname Miller?
8. The distance around a circle is called what?
9. Which mountain overlooks the South African city of Cape Town?
10. Which Shakespeare character is known as the 'Moor of Venice'?
11. What is the visual signalling code conducted with flags called?
12. What name is given to the part of the sundial that casts the shadow?
13. Born Doménikos Theotokópoulos in 1541, how is this painter, sculptor and architect of the Spanish Renaissance most widely known?
14. In computing what does the acronym RAM represent?
15. Ra, the Egyptian god of the sun has the head of which bird?

Answers

1. Joe Frazier 2. Halal 3. Istanbul 4. Prune
5. Labradoodle 6. Red 7. Dusty 8. Circumference
9. Table mountain 10. Othello 11. Semaphore
12. Gnomon 13. El Greco 14. Random Access Memory
15. Falcon

Quiz Eighty Four

1. In which US state is the Mount Rushmore National Memorial?
2. What type of creature is a John Dory?
3. The 38th Parallel demarcates the north and south of which country?
4. 'Colonel' Tom Parker was the manager of which famous singer?
5. The Nikkei index is the stock market index of which country?
6. What was the surname of American photography entrepreneur George, who popularized the use of roll film?
7. Which author wrote the 1945 novel 'Brideshead Revisited'?
8. Cannelloni is what type of food?
9. How many sides are there on a heptagon?
10. Born in Wyoming, USA in 1912, which painter and major figure in the abstract expressionist movement was dubbed 'Jack the Dripper'?
11. What was the name of the heavyweight boxer who retired in 1956 as the undefeated heavyweight champion of the world?
12. Chris Martin is lead singer of which rock band?
13. Which part of the human eye is affected by cataracts?
14. What is a rhinoceros horn made from?
15. Which English actor played Agent 006 Alec Trevelyan in the 1995 James Bond film 'GoldenEye'?

Answers

1. South Dakota 2. Fish 3. Korea 4. Elvis Presley
5. Japan 6. Eastman 7. Evelyn Waugh 8. Pasta 9. Seven
10. Jackson Pollock 11. Rocky Marciano 12. Coldplay
13. Lens 14. Keratin 15. Sean Bean

Quiz Eighty Five

1. Which American rock band recorded the 1976 album Hotel California?
2. Whose law states that 'Work expands so as to fit the time available for its completion'?
3. 'The Blue Boy' is a work by which English portrait and landscape painter, born in 1727?
4. Academy Award winning actress Julie Christie was born 17th April 1940 in which country?
5. What type of acid is used in car batteries?
6. What art form is a Japanese netsuke?
7. Luxor international airport is in which country?
8. What were the initials of the main security agency for the Soviet Union from 1954 until its break-up in 1991?
9. In photography what do the letters SLR stand for?
10. Russian revolutionary Leon Trotsky was assassinated on 21st August 1940, in which country?
11. What is the opposite of nocturnal?
12. What is the name of the sport played on broomsticks in the Harry Potter books?
13. Which Roman city was buried by volcanic ash following the eruption of Mount Vesuvius in 79 A.D?
14. In heraldic terms what colour is Argent?
15. What is a sheepshank?

Answers

1. The Eagles 2. Parkinson's 3. Thomas Gainsborough
4. India 5. Sulphuric 6. Sculpture 7. Egypt 8. KGB
9. Single lens reflex 10. Mexico 11. Diurnal 12. Quidditch
13. Pompeii 14. Silver 15. A knot

Quiz Eighty Six

1. According to the nursery rhyme, where did Doctor Foster go in a shower of rain?
2. In which sport are competitors forbidden to play left handed?
3. In the 2010 film 'The A-Team,' which actor played the role of Hannibal Smith?
4. Which actress played the role of May Day in the 1985 James Bond film 'A View to a Kill'?
5. In 1947 politician Jawaharlal Nehru became the first Prime Minister of which country?
6. English, Gordon and Irish are all breeds of what type of dog?
7. Dave Gilmore and Nick Mason were members of which English rock band?
8. Who was elected the first woman Prime Minister of Israel on 17th March 1969?
9. Kinshasa is the capital and the largest city of which democratic republic?
10. What name is given to an angle of more than 180 degrees but less than 360 degrees?
11. Which Australian mammal lays eggs?
12. What kind of tide appears at full Moon?
13. The designer Jimmy Choo specialises in what?
14. Tempera uses water and what to paint with?
15. Britain's Princess Diana died in a car crash in Paris, France on 31st August of which year?

Answers

1. Gloucester 2. Polo 3. Liam Neeson 4. Grace Jones
5. India 6. Setter 7. Pink Floyd 8. Golda Meir 9. Congo
10. Reflex 11. Duck-billed platypus 12. Spring tide
13. Shoes 14. Egg yolk 15. 1997

Quiz Eighty Seven

1. Which instrument is principally used in Boogie-woogie?
2. Racing driver Juan Manuel Fangio who dominated the first decade of Formula One racing, winning the World Drivers' Championship five times, was born in which country?
3. What is the more common name for the flower called helianthus?
4. Who was the lead vocalist with Thin Lizzy?
5. Which Charles Schulz created cartoon character made his first appearance in 1950?
6. Philip Pirrip is the central character in which Charles Dickens novel?
7. In the animated television series who is the youngest Simpson?
8. What is the colloquial name for the 1871 painting Arrangement in Grey and Black: Thc Artist's Mother?
9. Billy Bones and Benn Gunn are characters in which 1883 novel?
10. The Russian-born engineer Igor Sikorsky was a pioneer in the development of what form of transport?
11. What name is given to the tubular container used in archery to store arrows?
12. Cricketer Viv Richards represented which country in international cricket?
13. What is the world's largest continent?
14. In which state is the US President's retreat of Camp David?
15. The 1964 film 'The Sound of Music' was set in which country?

Answers

1. Piano 2. Argentina 3. Sunflower 4. Phil Lynott
5. Snoopy 6. Great Expectations 7. Maggie
8. Whistler's Mother 9. Treasure Island 10. Helicopter
11. Quiver 12. The West Indies 13. Asia 14. Maryland
15. Austria

Quiz Eighty Eight

1. Pop singer Ronan Keating first shot to fame as part of which Irish boy band?
2. Which planet is known for its Great Red Spot?
3. What is the first name of the Italian designer Versace, sister of Gianni?
4. What is the British equivalent of the American derby hat?
5. In which sport are there defensive positions called prime, tierce and octave?
6. Which human rights organisation founded by Peter Benenson in 1961 won the Nobel Prize in 1977?
7. In the animated television series 'Scooby Doo,' Dinkley was the surname of which character?
8. The St Valentine's Day Massacre took place in 1929 in which US city?
9. Which New Zealand city is known as The Garden City?
10. In which US state is the site of the US gold bullion depository of Fort Knox located?
11. Which comedy team included John Cleese, Michael Palin, Eric Idle, Graham Chapman and Terry Jones?
12. Which singer and actress in the early 1990s, she played Beth Brennan in the Australian soap opera 'Neighbours'?
13. What famous work of art, nearly 70 metres long and 50 centimetres tall, depicts events at the Battle of Hastings?
14. In which ocean would are The Maldives?
15. Pikachu is one of the species of creatures in which series of games?

Answers

1. Boyzone 2. Jupiter 3. Donatella 4. Bowler 5. Fencing
6. Amnesty International 7. Velma 8. Chicago
9. Christchurch 10. Kentucky 11. Monty Python
12. Natalie Imbruglia 13. The Bayeux Tapestry
14. Indian Ocean 15. Pokemon

Quiz Eighty Nine

1. Titan is the largest moon of which planet?
2. Which US city is nicknamed the windy city?
3. Idi Amin was president of which country from 1971 to 1979?
4. What do the letters DC stand for in the United States' capital Washington D.C.?
5. What did Clarice Cliff create?
6. Which lyricist wrote the words for the musicals 'My Fair Lady' and 'Camelot'?
7. The Live Aid dual-venue concerts held on 13th July 1985 were organised for raise funds for the relief of famine in which country?
8. How many wisdom teeth does an average adult have?
9. What three-letter term is used to describe one of the grades into which experienced judo contestants are divided?
10. At what racetrack is the British Formula One car race contested?
11. What is a 'Scotch Bonnet'?
12. Which British expedition leader died in Antarctica in March 1912?
13. Which ancient leader rode a horse called Bucephalus?
14. Emphysema affects which part of the human body?
15. What type of beverage is Lapsang souchong?

Answers

1. Saturn 2. Chicago 3. Uganda 4. District of Columbia 5. Pottery 6. Alan Jay Lerner 7. Ethiopia 8. Four 9. Dan 10. Silverstone Circuit 11. Chilli pepper 12. Robert Falcon Scott 13. Alexander the Great 14. Lungs 15. Tea

Quiz Ninety

1. The Carnation Revolution took place in which European country in April 1974?
2. In the 1942 film ‘Casablanca’ which actor played the role of Sam?
3. ‘Blonde on Blonde’ was a 1966 album release for which American singer-songwriter?
4. At which sport did Mark Spitz win seven Olympic gold medals in 1972?
5. What is an island formed by a volcanic eruption called?
6. What is the medical name for the shin bone?
7. What does the Olympic motto ‘Citius, Altius, Fortius’ mean in English?
8. In which country is the Great Sandy Desert?
9. What type of animal is a samoyed?
10. What number system uses only the digits 1 and 0?
11. What does an ammeter measure?
12. In which Jules Verne novel of 1873 does Passe-partout appear?
13. What sort of pastry is used to make profiteroles?
14. Who recorded albums titled ‘Dangerous,’ ‘Thriller’ and ‘Bad’?
15. In a typical deck of playing cards which suits are red?

Answers

1. Portugal 2. Dooley Wilson 3. Bob Dylan 4. Swimming 5. Atoll 6. Tibia 7. Faster, Higher, Stronger 8. Australia 9. Dog 10. Binary 11. Electric current 12. Around the World in Eighty Days 13. Choux 14. Michael Jackson 15. Hearts and Diamonds

Quiz Ninety One

1. What is the capital city of Latvia?
2. In which year did the Russian Revolution take place?
3. By what name is the fictional character Lord Greystoke better known?
4. Which punctuation mark does an American call a period?
5. What musical instrument did Fats Waller play?
6. Which item of clothing was created by French designer Louis Reard in 1946?
7. Which British racing driver, who died in an air crash in 1975, was twice Formula One World Champion?
8. What type of precious stone is the Koh-I-Noor?
9. Which vegetable is known as the eggplant in the United States?
10. Which car manufacturer uses a logo consisting of three diamonds?
11. Which continent has the most countries?
12. In which sport is a dolly known as an easy catch?
13. Which Nobel Prize-winning English playwright wrote the plays 'The Birthday Party' and 'The Caretaker'?
14. What is the only chemical element that has a three-letter name?
15. Which actor played the role of Professor Severus Snape in the Harry Potter films?

Answers

1. Riga 2. 1917 3. Tarzan 4. Full stop 5. Piano
6. Bikini 7. Graham Hill 8. Diamond 9. Aubergine
10. Mitsubishi 11. Africa 12. Cricket 13. Harold Pinter
14. Tin 15. Alan Rickman

Quiz Ninety Two

1. The Hudson River flows through which American city?
2. Venison is meat obtained from which animal?
3. The Chinese Gooseberry is another name for which fruit?
4. Which actor played the title role in the 2002 film 'Billy Elliot'?
5. What is the name of the lioness in the book Joy Adamson 'Born Free'?
6. In which year did London first host the Summer Olympic Games?
7. Which Commonwealth country lies off the south east coast of India?
8. In which Asian country is Mount Fuji?
9. Of the original seven wonders of the ancient world, which is the only one still surviving?
10. In Ancient Greek literature, who wrote the epic poems 'Iliad' and 'Odyssey'?
11. At 2,290 miles long, what is the name of the longest river in Europe?
12. In the periodic table of elements, which element has the symbol As?
13. How many players make up a team in Ice Hockey?
14. Diamonds are a form of which chemical element?
15. What is the Decalogue usually called?

Answers

1. New York 2. Deer 3. Kiwi fruit 4. Jamie Bell 5. Elsa 6. 1908 7. Sri Lanka 8. Japan 9. Great Pyramid of Giza 10. Homer 11. Volga 12. Arsenic 13. Six 14. Carbon 15. The Ten Commandments

Quiz Ninety Three

1. Quicksilver is the alternative name of which element?
2. What are lines called which always have the same distance between them?
3. Which republic is the third largest island in the Mediterranean Sea?
4. What was the name of the American film director and screenwriter who Julie Andrews married in 1969?
5. 'Thanks for the Memory' was the signature tine of which comedian, singer and actor, who died at the age of 100 in 2003?
6. On 12th August 1851 Isaac Singer patented the first practical and efficient version of what device?
7. In science what are the three states of matter?
8. Which instrument with a rotating telescope is used in surveying to measure horizontal and vertical angles?
9. What is a female swan called?
10. Which creature's name was derived from two Greek words that mean terrible lizard?
11. In the Harry Potter books what are the names of the four houses of Hogwarts School?
12. In which American television drama did Idris Elba play the role of Russell 'Stringer' Bell?
13. A rhombus has how many sides?
14. What sport involves stones and a house?
15. Warsaw is the capital city of which country?

Answers

1. Mercury 2. Parallel 3. Cyprus 4. Blake Edwards 5. Bob Hope 6. Sewing machine 7. Solid, liquid, and gas 8. Theodolite 9. Pen 10. Dinosaur 11. Gryffindor, Slytherin, Ravenclaw and Hufflepuff 12. The Wire 13. Four 14. Curling 15. Poland

Quiz Ninety Four

1. The name of which sport means ‘empty hand’ in Japanese?
2. Which Rodgers & Hammerstein musical features the songs, ‘Getting To Know You’ and ‘Shall We Dance’?
3. What is the capital city of the US state of Arizona?
4. Which radiation belt around the earth was named after an American space scientist?
5. What is the name of The Rolling Stones’ drummer?
6. Which actor played the role of Hagrid in the Harry Potter films?
7. What is a female deer called?
8. In which battle of June 1876 did General Custer have his ‘Last Stand’?
9. ‘It was a bright cold day in April, and the clocks were striking thirteen,’ are the opening lines of which George Orwell novel?
10. What is the outermost region of the Earth’s atmosphere called?
11. In which Asian city are the Petronas Twin Towers?
12. What is the name of the mountain ranges that separates France and Spain?
13. Which is the only country in the world that holds the title of Grand Duchy?
14. What is the name of the school in the film ‘Grease’?
15. Which Australian tennis player was nicknamed The Rockhampton Rocket, after his Queensland birthplace?

Answers

1. Karate 2. The King and I 3. Phoenix 4. (James)
Van Allen Belt 5. Charlie Watts 6. Robbie Coltrane
7. Doe 8. The Battle of Little Bighorn 9. 1984
10. Exosphere 11. Kuala Lumpur 12. The Pyrenees
13. Luxembourg 14. Rydell High 15. Rod Laver

Quiz Ninety Five

1. Who is the father of American actor and rapper Jaden Smith?
2. In the English nursery rhyme, who was born on a Monday and died on a Sunday?
3. Which spice comes from the dried stigmas of crocus flowers?
4. What is the name of the ice cream dessert which is encased in meringue?
5. Which significant line of latitude passes through Kenya?
6. How many forwards are there in a rugby union team?
7. In the 1939 film 'The Wizard of Oz' what is Dorothy's dog called?
8. In 2001 the name of which city was changed to Kolkata?
9. Which famous actress said 'Keep a diary and one day it'll keep you'?
10. On 8th November 1895 what did German/Dutch mechanical engineer and physicist, Wilhelm Röntgen, discover?
11. Which river flows through the Grand Canyon?
12. Was US President Bill Clinton a Democrat or a Republican?
13. Which scientific instrument is used to measure atmospheric pressure?
14. Established in 1592 what is the oldest university in Ireland?
15. Which is the only British county with two coastlines?

Answers

1. Will Smith 2. Solomon Grundy 3. Saffron 4. Baked Alaska 5. Equator 6. Eight 7. Toto 8. Calcutta 9. Mae West 10. X-rays 11. Colorado 12. Democrat 13. Barometer 14. Trinity College, Dublin 15. Devon

Quiz Ninety Six

1. Which musical features the song 'Brush up Your Shakespeare'?
2. Born in 1941, what is the stage name of musician Robert Zimmerman?
3. Which father and daughter co-starred in the 1973 film 'Paper Moon'?
4. '1984' was the final film of which Welsh actor?
5. Capitoline Hill is the tallest hill in which city?
6. Which actor was married to Mildred Harris, Lita Grey, Paulette Goddard and Oona O'Neill?
7. In which country is the Aswan Dam?
8. What is the largest island in the Mediterranean?
9. What species of ape are native to the Rock of Gibraltar?
10. Which wading bird was sacred to the ancient Egyptians?
11. Which is the fourth letter of the Greek alphabet?
12. Which English mathematician, astronomer, and physicist, on 4th January 1643, discovered gravity?
13. What name is given to the hobby of stamp collecting?
14. Which metal can be described as ferrous?
15. What type of creature is a tarantula?

Answers

1. Kiss Me Kate 2. Bob Dylan 3. Ryan and Tatum O'Neal 4. Richard Burton 5. Rome 6. Charlie Chaplin 7. Egypt 8. Sicily 9. Barbary 10. Ibis 11. Delta 12. Sir Isaac Newton 13. Philately 14. Iron 15. Spider

Quiz Ninety Seven

1. L is the Roman numeral for what number?
2. The fictional character Captain Arthur J. M. Hastings, OBE, is the companion-chronicler and best friend of which detective?
3. Douglas is the capital of which British island?
4. Graphite, used in pencil leads, is a form of which chemical element?
5. Who won the Academy Award for Best Actor in 1999 for his role as Lester Burnham in 'American Beauty'?
6. What is the full name of the country known as the UAE?
7. What is the hardest substance in the human body?
8. Which historical character was assassinated on the Ides of March?
9. Which rock group includes bass player Adam Clayton?
10. What is the name of the chocolate factory owner in 'Charlic and the Chocolate Factory'?
11. Developed by James Dyson and launched in 1993, the DC01 was a what?
12. Joan of Arc is also known as the Maid of where?
13. Who was the only woman to win two Nobel prizes?
14. In which country is the Dead Sea?
15. What was the currency in Italy before the euro?

Answers

1. 50 2. Hercule Poirot 3. Isle of Man 4. Carbon
5. Kevin Spacey 6. United Arab Emirates 7. Tooth
enamel 8. Julius Caesar 9. U2 10. Willy Wonka
11. Vacuum cleaner 12. Orleans 13. Marie Curie
14. Israel 15. Lira

Quiz Ninety Seven

1. Something described as 'tactile' means that it relates to which of the senses?
2. What type of animal is a Suffolk Punch?
3. Which Norwegian artist painted the 'The Scream'?
4. Which two South American countries are landlocked?
5. Brass is an alloy of which two metals?
6. The leaves of the eucalyptus tree are the principle food of what marsupial?
7. In which Italian city is the Uffizi Gallery?
8. Which nut is used to flavour traditional Bakewell Tart?
9. What is Bombay Duck?
10. In which country can the city of Durban be found?
11. In which ocean are the Seychelles located?
12. In which country do Shinkansen 'bullet trains' operate?
13. Where do arboreal animals live?
14. Who did American settler John Rolfe marry in 1614?
15. How many carats are there in pure gold?

Answers

1. Touch 2. Horse 3. Edvard Munch 4. Bolivia and Paraguay 5. Copper and zinc 6. The koala 7. Florence 8. Almond 9. Fish 10. South Africa 11. Indian Ocean 12. Japan 13. In trees 14. Pocahontas 15. 24

Quiz Ninety Eight

1. Which famous US building was officially known as The Executive Mansion until 1901?
2. Which actor, whose films include 'Giant,' died in a car accident on 30th September 1955?
3. Under what name did H. C. McNeile write the Bulldog Drummond novels?
4. How many years apart are the summer Olympic Games?
5. Which English author wrote the 1871 poem 'The Owl and the Pussycat'?
6. In which country is the Bay of Pigs?
7. The 1945 film 'Spellbound,' starred Gregory Peck and Ingrid Bergman; who directed it?
8. OPEC stands for the Organization of Petrol Exporting what?
9. What is the official language of Brazil?
10. Which member of the cat family is the fastest animal on land?
11. Which Scottish-born scientist and inventor is credited with patenting the first practical telephone?
12. In which South American country is the Atacama Desert?
13. The small republic of San Marino is completely surrounded by which larger country?
14. Poland's only coastline is on which sea?
15. Which reggae music legend was backed by The Wailers?

Answers

1. The White House 2. James Dean 3. Sapper 4. Four
5. Edward Lear 6. Cuba 7. Alfred Hitchcock 8. Countries
9. Portuguese 10. Cheetah 11. Alexander Graham Bell
12. Chile 13. Italy 14. Baltic Sea 15. Bob Marley

Quiz Ninety Nine

1. Which English poet and literary critic wrote the 1816 poem 'Kubla Khan'?
2. In 1968 Sirhan Bishara Sirhan was convicted of the assassination of which U.S. Senator?
3. The Golden Bear was the nickname of which retired American professional golfer?
4. Who, in 1670, is credited with inventing champagne?
5. Russian revolutionary Fanny Kaplan tried to assassinate which leader in August 1918?
6. What word is given to describe last but one in a series of things?
7. How many candles does The Hanukkah menorah have?
8. What is the world's largest reptile?
9. Which German statesman who as the first post-war Chancellor of Germany (West Germany) from 1949 to 1963?
10. Which Irish province comprises the counties of Clare, Cork, Kerry, Tipperary, Limerick and Waterford?
11. What 1980s television programme starred Tyne Daly and Sharon Gless?
12. What word is applied to someone who is able to use their right and left hands equally well?
13. Which British speed record breaker was killed trying to break his own water speed record on Coniston Water in January 1967?
14. What name is given to the triangular part of a horse's hoof?
15. Following the death of Richard Harris, which actor took over the role of Dumbledore in the third film of the Harry Potter series?

Answers

1. Samuel Taylor Coleridge 2. Robert F. Kennedy 3. Jack Nicklaus 4. Dom Perignon 5. Vladimir Lenin 6. Penultimate 7. Nine 8. Crocodile 9. Konrad Adenauer 10. Munster 11. Cagney & Lacey 12. Ambidextrous 13. Donald Campbell 14. Frog 15. Michael Gambon

Quiz One Hundred

1. Which British crime writer wrote six novels under the nom-de-plume Mary Westmacott?
2. Which actor played the role of Alan Turing in the 2014 film 'The Imitation Game'?
3. How many countries border France?
4. Who did Jacqueline Lee Bouvier marry on 12th September 1953?
5. British sportsman Henry Copper was associated with which sport?
6. Boy George is the leading singer of which Brit Award-winning pop band?
7. Stratosphere, Earthquake, Tempest and Ice are variants of which computer game?
8. Lac Leman is the French customary name for which lake shared between France and Switzerland?
9. Which company developed the Xbox 360?
10. Video game series is set in and around the world of Azeroth?
11. Antonio Vivaldi's 'Four Seasons' was written for which instrument?
12. Which two British monarchs have celebrated a diamond jubilee?
13. In snooker what colour is the cue ball?
14. The Mariana Trench, the deepest part of the world's oceans, is located in which ocean?
15. Into which body of water does the Danube river flow?

Answers

1. Agatha Christie 2. Benedict Cumberbatch 3. Eight
4. John F. Kennedy 5. Boxing 6. Culture Club 7. Tetris
8. Lake Geneva 9. Microsoft 10. Warcraft 11. Violin
12. Victoria and Elizabeth II 13. White 14. Pacific
15. Black Sea

Printed in Great Britain
by Amazon

59942759R00061